EARL MOUNTBATTEN OF BURMA, 1900–1979

Historiography and Annotated Bibliography

Recent Titles in
Bibliographies of British Statesmen

Lord Curzon, 1839–1925: A Bibliography
James G. Parker

Lord Nelson, 1758–1805: A Bibliography
Leonard W. Cowie

The Duke of Wellington, 1769–1852: A Bibliography
Michael Partridge

Charles James Fox, 1749–1806: A Bibliography
David Schweitzer

George Grenville, 1712–1770: A Bibliography
Rory T. Cornish

William Wilberforce, 1759–1833: A Bibliography
Leonard W. Cowie

Margaret Thatcher: A Bibliography
Faysal Mikdadi

William Pitt, Earl of Chatham, 1708–1778: A Bibliography
Karl W. Schweizer

Lord Palmerston, 1784–1865: A Bibliography
Michael S. Partridge and Karen E. Partridge

Edmund Burke, 1729–1797: A Bibliography
Leonard W. Cowie

Sir Robert Peel, 1788–1850: A Bibliography
Leonard W. Cowie

The Duke of Newcastle, 1693–1768 and Henry Pelham, 1694–1754: A Bibliography
P. J. Kulisheck

EARL MOUNTBATTEN OF BURMA, 1900–1979

Historiography and Annotated Bibliography

Eugene L. Rasor

BIBLIOGRAPHIES OF
BRITISH STATESMEN, NO. 21

MYRON J. SMITH, JR., SERIES ADVISER

Greenwood Press
Westport, Connecticut • London

Library of Congress Cataloging-in-Publication Data

Rasor, Eugene L., 1936–
    Earl Mountbatten of Burma, 1900–1979 : historiography and
annotated bibliography / Eugene L. Rasor.
      p. cm.—(Bibliographies of British statesmen, ISSN
1056–5515 ; no. 21)
    Includes bibliographical references and index.
    ISBN 0–313–28876–3 (alk. paper)
    1. Mountbatten of Burma, Louis Mountbatten, Earl, 1900–1979—
Bibliography. 2. Great Britain—History, Naval—20th century—
Bibliography. 3. Statesmen—Great Britain—Biography—
Bibliography. 4. India—History—1947- —Bibliography. I. Title.
II. Series.
Z8602.194.R37   1998
[DA89. 1.M59]
016.941082′092—dc21   97–49964

British Library Cataloguing in Publication Data is available.

Library of Congress Catalog Card Number: 97–49964
ISBN: 0–313–28876–3
ISSN: 1056–5515

First published in 1998

Greenwood Press, 88 Post Road West, Westport, CT 06881
An imprint of Greenwood Publishing Group, Inc.

Printed in the United States of America

The paper used in this book complies with the
Permanent Paper Standard issued by the National
Information Standards Organization (Z39.48–1984).

10 9 8 7 6 5 4 3 2

To Rosemary and Bryan Ricketts

Edge
Gloucestershire
United Kingdom

Contents

Acknowledgments   *ix*

Abbreviations   *xi*

Chronology   *xiii*

PART I: HISTORIOGRAPHICAL NARRATIVE

CHAPTER 1   Introduction and Biographical Essay   1

CHAPTER 2   Manuscript and Archival Resources   5

CHAPTER 3   Biographical Works about Earl Mountbatten and Lady
             Mountbatten   12

CHAPTER 4   Works about Mountbatten and the Royal Family   17

CHAPTER 5   Works about Mountbatten and the Royal Navy   21

CHAPTER 6   Works about Mountbatten and World War II   26

CHAPTER 7   Works about Mountbatten, Viceroy and Governor-
             General of India   39

CHAPTER 8   Works about Mountbatten, First Sea Lord and Chief of
             Defense Staff   45

CHAPTER 9   Retirement and Death of Earl Mountbatten   49

PART II: ANNOTATED BIBLIOGRAPHY   57

Author Index   129

Subject Index   135

Acknowledgments

This historiographical and bibliographical survey on Earl Mountbatten of Burma is a complete reference and research guide for the use of all levels of students and scholars and all persons interested in international developments in the twentieth century. It reviews all of the important primary and secondary sources concerned with Earl Mountbatten of Burma.

This book is dedicated to dear friends and generous hosts who have consistently facilitated the research and writing of this and other works: Rosemary and Bryan Ricketts of Edge, Gloucestershire.

Every bibliographer is indebted to hundreds of librarians, archivists, colleagues, and friends like the Ricketts who have provided assistance in acquiring access to and information about pertinent publications, journals, official documents, dissertations, and other materials. Friends and family have facilitated the processes of traveling to resource centers and libraries and conducting research. I am no exception. All is greatly appreciated.

I am indebted to several funding agencies, university and public libraries, research centers, and persons. Generous provisions for sabbatical leaves and financial assistance from the Mellon Foundation, the McConnell Fellowship, Faculty Enrichment Fund, and the Faculty Travel Grant, have come from Emory and Henry College, Mednick Fellowships through the Virginia Foundation of Independent Colleges, a National Endowment for the Humanities Summer Institute, and from the General Douglas MacArthur Foundation, Norfolk, Virginia.

Educational institutions, research centers, and private and public libraries to which I am much indebted include, in the United States, the Library of Congress, the General Douglas MacArthur Memorial Museum and Archive, Norfolk, VA, the George C. Marshall Library, Lexington, VA, the libraries of the U.S. Army Military History Institute and the U.S. Army War College, Carlisle Barracks, PA, the U.S. Naval Academy, Annapolis, MD, the U.S. Naval War College, Newport, RI, and the university libraries of Brown, Chicago, Duke,

Emory and Henry College, Georgetown, Indiana, Kentucky, Maryland, North Carolina, North Carolina State, Old Dominion, Tennessee, Virginia, and Virginia Tech; in Great Britain, the British Library, the Public Record Office, Kew, the Institute of Historical Research, London, the City of Portsmouth Library, and the university libraries of Cambridge, East Anglia, Edinburgh, London, and Southampton, where the Mountbatten papers are housed.   The contributions of individual persons, colleagues, friends, and family members have been essential and are much appreciated.   James Controvich, author of the bibliography covering the Central Pacific theater in this same series, has provided incisive critiques which have been extremely helpful. Others who have provided assistance in a variety of ways include Colin Baxter, Michael Galgano, Robin Higham, Clayton James, Archer Jones, Thomas Morris, Malcolm Muir, Carol Petillo, Norman Pollock, Jack Roper, Michael Schaller, George Stevenson, Jon Sumida, Betty Young, and Charles Young. Sharie Wilson puts it all together.

As always, my family have been loving and supportive. What would I do without them? In particular, my wife Claire has contributed in the most essential details and in all other ways.

Myron J. Smith, Jr., Series Advisor, Greenwood Press, is always receptive and helpful. Mildred Vasan and Cynthia Harris, Senior Editors, Greenwood Publishing Group, have been indulgent and have assisted in numerous ways.

Abbreviations

NOTE: When there is repetition, space can be saved by the use of abbreviations. In most cases only the first name of the publisher has been included: for example, Random for Random House, Houghton for Houghton-Mifflin, Little for Little, Brown, and Arms for Arms and Armour. Some names of publishers have been shortened: NIP for Naval Institute Press, GPO for Government Printing Office, HMSO for His or Her Majesty's Stationery Office, Brassey for Brassey's, Jane for Jane's, St. Martin for St. Martin's, Putnam for Putnam's, UNCP for University of North Carolina Press, and USCP for University of South Carolina Press. Abbreviations for various armed services and associated organizations have been used: RN for Royal Navy, USN for United States Navy, USMC for United States Marine Corps, RAF for Royal Air Force, and RN for Royal Navy. Titles of journals, names of publishers, names of major cities often cited, and other items have been abbreviated as follows:

ABDA or ABDACOM = American, British, Dutch, Australian Command
AQ&DJ = Army Quarterly and Defence Journal
AUSWARMEM = Australian War Memorial
CANHISREV = Canadian History Review
C-B-I = China-Burma-India theater
COHQ = Combined Operations Headquarters
diss = dissertation
FDR = Franklin Delano Roosevelt
HISTOD = History Today
HJ = Historical Journal
HMSO = His or Her Majesty's Stationery Office
IWM = Imperial War Museum
IMPWARMUSREV = Imperial War Museum Review
INTHISREV = International History Review
JCONHIS = Journal of Contemporary History

JI&CH = Journal of Imperial and Commonwealth History
JMILHIS = Journal of Military History
JRUSI = Journal of the Royal United Services Institution
JSTRASTU = Journal of Strategic Studies
LRPG = Long Range Penetration Group
MM = Mariner's Mirror
MILAFF = Military Affairs
MILREV = Military Review
WWTSA NEWS = Newsletter of the World War Two Studies Association
n.m. = no month
NIP = Naval Institute Press
NIPROC = Proceedings of the U.S. Naval Institute
NRS = Navy Records Society
NWCR = Naval War College Review
NY = New York City
PACHISREV = Pacific Historical Review
Ph.D. diss = unpublished Doctor of Philosophy dissertation
PRO = Public Record Office
RAF = Royal Air Force
RN = Royal Navy
SAC = Supreme Allied Comander
SAS = Special Air Squadron
SBS = Special Boat Squadron
SEAC = Southeast or South-East Asia Command
SOG = Small Operational Group
trans. = translated
UP = University Press
USARMYWWII = U.S. Army History of World War II
USN = United States Navy
UWC = United World Colleges
Wash = Washington, DC
W&S = War and Society

Chronology

Note: all entries apply to Earl Mountbatten unless otherwise stated.

1900-1979

25 June 1900, Born, Frogmore House, Windsor.

28 November 1901, Edwina Ashley, the future Lady Mountbatten, born in London.

1905-1909, Education at home and at Macpherson's Gymnastic School, Sloane Street, London.

1910-1913, Locker's Park Preparatory School.

May 1913-1914, Naval Training College, Osborne.

October 1914, Prince Louis of Battenberg resigned as First Sea Lord.

November 1914-1916, Royal Naval College, Dartmouth.

1914-1921, Residence at Osborne House, Isle of Wight.

July 1916, Midshipman, HMS LION.

February 1916-1917, HMS QUEEN ELIZABETH; a month aboard submarine K6.

June 1917, Name change, from Battenberg to Mountbatten; King George V changed name of royal family, House of Hanover to House of Windsor.

July 1918, Promoted to Sub-Lieutenant; to HMS P.31.

1919-1920, Cambridge University, Cambridge, to Lieutenant.

1920, HMS RENOWN.

1921-1922, World tours with Edward, Prince of Wales.

1921, Edwina Ashley inherited a fortune eventually including Broadlands and Classiebawn Castle; to HMS REPULSE.

14 February 1922, Proposal of marriage to Edwina in India.

18 July 1922, Marriage at St. Margaret's Church, Westminster; honeymoon in the U.S., to Hollywood.

1923, HMS REVENGE.

14 February 1924, Daughter Patricia born.

1924-1926, Signal School, Portsmouth and to Royal Naval College, Greenwich.

1926-1929, Mediterranean Fleet as Signals and Wireless Officer; promoted to Lieutenant Commander.

1929, Daughter Pamela born.

1929-1931, Senior Instructor, Signals School.

1931-1933, Mediterranean Fleet, Wireless Officer.

1931, As MARCO, wrote Introduction to Polo.

1932, Promoted to Commander.

1934, Command, destroyer HMS DARING.

1935, Command, destroyer HMS WISHART.

July 1935, Mountbatten before Larken Committee on the Communications System of the Royal Navy.

1939, Promoted to Captain; to command, HMS KELLY, and Fifth Destroyer Flotilla.

September 1939, European/Atlantic war began; KELLY in Norwegian and Crete campaigns; damaged several times; Winston Churchill returned to the Admiralty as First Lord; Edwina began career, St. John Ambulance Brigade.

1940, Awarded D.S.O.; appointed Commodore.

10 May 1940, Churchill as Prime Minister

June 1940, Creation of Directorate of Raiding Operations.

17 July 1940, Roger Keyes, Director of Combined Operations; Commandos created.

23 May 1941, Battle of Crete; HMS KELLY sunk off Crete.

1941, Appointed command, HMS ILLUSTRIOUS; to Newport News, Virginia.

17 October 1941, Keyes removed, COHQ.

27 October 1941, Mountbatten, Director, Combined Operations, promoted to Acting Vice Admiral.

December 1941, Vaagso (Norway) raid.

March 1942, Chief of Combined Operations; member of British Chiefs of Staff Committee, to 1943.

27-28 March 1942, St. Nazaire raid.

March-April 1942, Sir Stafford Cripps Mission to India.

June 1942, Rehearsal for Dieppe raid.

July 1942, Edwina, Superintendent-in-Chief, St. John Ambulance Brigade.

19 August 1942, Dieppe raid.

August 1943, Quebec Conference; Supreme Allied Commander, South-East Asia Command (SAC SEAC); Acting Admiral and courtsey ranks, General and Air Marshal; to 1946.

December 1943, Cairo Conference: FDR, Churchill, Chiang Kai-shek, Mountbatten.

24 March 1944, Orde Wingate killed in air crash.

April 1944, SAC SEAC HQ moved to Kandy, Ceylon.

June 1944, Japan launched offensive for invasion of India; second Burma campaign to end of war, September 1945.

July 1945, Potsdam Conference; Mountbatten present; SEAC area extended; Labor won British election; Attlee government to 1951.

15 August 1945, Japanese announced surrender; Edwina led rescue operation of Allied Prisoners of War, Southeast Asia.

12 September 1945, Accepted surrender of Japanese forces, Singapore; elevated to title of Viscount, reverted to Rear Admiral.

1945-1946, OPERATION MASTERDOM - British General Gracey and British force arrive in Indochina (Saigon); facilitated return of French colonial administration; handover to civil government in Burma.

1946, Patricia married Baron Brabourne; Mountbatten made Honorary Fellow, Christ's College, Cambridge University; Mountbatten created Viscount.

December 1946, Appointed Viceroy of India.

20 March 1947, India as Viceroy.

15 August 1947, Transfer of power and separation in India; much violence and displacement of millions.

1947, Aung San of Burma assassinated.

1947, Created Earl Mountbatten of Burma; Edwina correspondence and relationship with Nehru, to 1960.

August 1947-June 1948, Governor-General of India.

November 1947, Situation stabilized in India and Pakistan.

30 January 1948, Gandhi assassinated.

21 June 1948, Departed India; reverted to Rear Admiral.

1948-1949, Commander, 1st Cruiser Squadron, Mediterranean Fleet; to Vice Admiral.

June 1950-1952, Fourth Sea Lord, at Admiralty, Whitehall; Edwina to Superintendent-in-Chief, St. John Ambulance Brigade Overseas.

1951-1955, Conservatives won election, Churchill returned as PM.

1952-1954, Commander-in-Chief, Mediterranean Fleet; Supreme Allied Commander, NATO, Mediterranean; to Admiral; personal Aide-de-Camp to Queen Elizabeth.

April 1955, Anthony Eden replaced Churchill as PM.

1955-1959, First Sea Lord.

1956, Events in Egypt: American offer to assist in Aswan High Dam; then offer withdrawn; Nasser nationalized Suez Canal; later concluded arms deal with Soviet Russia.

October 1956, Admiral of the Fleet.

30 October-November, British-French-Israel planned and executed Suez campaign; U.S. objected; British and French withdrew.

December, Clearance of Suez Canal began.

January 1957, Macmillan replaced Eden as PM; Defence White Paper: Great Britain to develop own independent nuclear capability.

July 1959, Chief of Defense Staff; beginning of consolidation of armed forces.

21 February 1960, Edwina died on Borneo, body returned and buried at sea near Portsmouth.

1960, Pamela married David Hicks.

1962, CDS term expired, requested to remain to 1964, then again to 1965.

December 1962, Nassau Agreement, Great Britain obtained Polaris missiles from the U.S.

1964, Ministry of Defense created.

1965, Defense White Paper.

July 1965, Retired as Chief of Defense Staff; appointed Governor of Isle of Wight, Colonel of Life Guards, Colonel Commandant of Royal Marines, etc.

1966-1967, Presentation of 13-part TV Documentary, BBC; report on Prison Security for the Home Secretary.

11 July 1967, Centennial Address, Empire Club of Canada.

May 1968, Cecil King Affair, an aborted plan to dismiss Harold Wilson as PM and replace him with a coalition government headed by Mountbatten.

1978, Broadlands Estate opened to the public.

May 1979, Speech at Strasbourg for arms control.

1979, Summer at Classiebawn Castle, County Sligo.

27 August 1979, Bank Holiday. Monday, 11:45 AM, Mountbatten assassinated, blown up in a yacht by a remote control bomb actuated by IRA operatives. Next several days:
--body lay in state, Romsey Abbey.
--body lay in state, St. James Palace.
--funeral, Westminster Abbey.
--special train from Waterloo Station to Romsey.
--burial, Romsey Abbey near Broadlands Estate.

Part I

HISTORIOGRAPHICAL NARRATIVE

1

Introduction and Biographical Essay

The format of Earl Mountbatten of Burma, 1900-1979: Historiography and Annotated Bibliography includes a chronological table, an extensive historiographical narrative section incorporating a survey of all of the important literature by and about Earl Mountbatten, an annotated bibliography section, and indexes, author and subject. The narrative will integrate historical and biographical events, criticisms, evaluations and assessments of the literature, and appropriate observations. "The Literature" means published books, monographs, official histories, government publications, memoirs, diaries, dissertations, bibliographies, pertinent articles from journals and periodicals, collections of unpublished papers and letters, various manuscripts and manuscript collections, archival and research locations and germane holdings, published and broadcast interviews, all in English and other Western languages. TV documentaries, films, important paintings, and sculptures also will be included.

This historiographical survey and annotated bibliography of Earl Mountbatten of Burma was planned and prepared so as to round out a series of similar publications. Mountbatten served as Supreme Allied Commander, Southeast Asia Command, one of three major command theaters of the Asian/Pacific war of World War II. By most definitions the Southeast Asia Command was equivalent to the China-Burma-India theater. In the Bibliographies of Battles and Leaders series of Greenwood Press, all three theaters are covered: The Central Pacific Campaign by James Controvich [77], published in 1990, The Southwest Pacific Campaign by Eugene Rasor [341], published in 1996, and The China-Burma-India Campaign, forthcoming by Rasor [339]. Rasor has also completed a volume on the first major offensive campaign of the war, The Solomon Islands Campaign. Two of the three supreme Allied commanders of theaters are now covered, both by Rasor [340]: for the Southwest Pacific, General Douglas MacArthur, published in 1994, and for China-Burma-India, Earl Mountbatten of Burma. It is in Greenwood's Bibliographies of British Statesmen series because Mountbatten was so important in international, imperial, and political matters in addition to the war. A thorough study of publications by and about the third commander, U.S. Admiral Chester Nimitz of the Pacific Ocean Area, including the Central Pacific, led to the conclusion that there was insufficient material published by and about Nimitz to warrant a book-length bibliography.

There are quantitative and qualitative features of the book. Specifically, general histories, monographs, bibliographies, reference works, official histories, published reports, government documents, unpublished dissertations, scholarly and some popular articles, oral histories, proceedings of conferences and symposiums, fiction, film, art, and poetry are included. All of that material will then be incorporated, reviewed, evaluated, analyzed, critiqued, and integrated into the overall literature about Mountbatten, and will be placed in the context of the twentieth century.

The bibliographer and the scholar who formulate historiographical surveys of the literature on a topic face limitations. Only what has been published can be appraised and assessed. Gaps exist in that literature and further research and writing are needed. These deficiences and opportunities for more study and publication are pointed out in the final chapter of the Historiographical Narrative section.

Finally, <u>Earl Mountbatten of Burma</u> is divided into two major sections for the convenience of the reader and researcher. Part I, the Historiographical Narrative section, includes a general survey and review of everything which is collected and incorporated into Part II, the Annotated Bibliography section, consisting of 450 annotated entries. Part I, the Historiographical Narrative section, features critical analysis, critiques, evaluation, assessment, and integration into the overall literature. A conscious effort has been made to incorporate analytical and qualitative judgments. In each of the chapters and subdivisions, the best, most useful, most praised works are reviewed early in the presentations, generally in some detail. Lesser, complementary, and supplementary works are included but with less emphasis and comment. Every one of the 450 numbered entries in Part II, the Annotated Bibliography section, is incorporated, integrated, and placed in context in Part I, the Historiographical Narrative section.

The Annotated Bibliography section brings together 450 entries. It is structured alphabetically so that, in most cases, the first letter of the last name of the author is the key. Each is numbered in order, 1-450. Several ways of cross-referencing, integration, linkage, and the standard indexes of author and subject have been incorporated. Every pertinent citation in Part I, the Historiographical Narrative section, is designated by a bracketed numbered entry, "[109]", taken from Part II, the Annotated Bibliography section.

This historiographical survey and annotated bibliography is about Admiral of the Fleet the Right Honorable Louis Francis Albert Victor Nicholas, first Earl Mountbatten of Burma, KG, PC, GCB, OM, GCSI, GCIE, GCVO,

DSO, FRS, Hon. DCL, and Hon. LLD. The Victor and the Albert were included in the formal name to fulfill a request from Queen Victoria. Nicknames were common among royalty and Nicky was first selected. That led to confusion with the Tsar of Russia and "Dickie" was finally settled upon. It remained his nickname until death. Details about the titles and honors of Earl Mountbatten and Lady Mountbatten and nicknames are included in the final chapter.

Mountbatten was the second son to Admiral of the Fleet Prince Louis of Battenberg, subsequently the first Marquess of Milford Haven, and the Princess Victoria of Hesse, granddaughter of Queen Victoria.

Mountbatten was an interesting, influential, renowned, glamorous, and controversial figure in naval, military, political, international, monarchical, and social affairs. Eric Grove has called him "perhaps the most remarkable naval officer of the twentieth century" (Review of Ziegler [445], Mountbatten, 1985). Eric Grove was director of the Mountbatten Center of Southampton University in Great Britain. That is the location of the Broadlands and Mountbatten Papers.

Mountbatten was born at Frogmore House, Windsor, on 25 June 1900, son of Prince Louis of Battenberg, Admiral, First Sea Lord of the Admiralty (1912-1914) at the beginning of World War I. The Battenbergs descended from the Grand Dukes of Hesse. Earl Mountbatten was a great-grandson of Queen Victoria and nephew of Tsar Nicholas II of Russia. Queen Victoria held the baby Mountbatten at the christening. He was cousin to Kings Edward VIII and George VI of Great Britain. He attended the Royal Naval College, Dartmouth and Cambridge University. A description of Frogmore House, located within the Home Park, Windsor Castle, was by Hugh Roberts [348]. It was opened to the public in 1990. The Mountbattens lived at Osborne House on the Isle of Wight, 1914-1921. Arnold Florence [130] wrote about visits there by Queen Victoria, foreword by Earl Mountbatten.

The Battenbergs officially changed their name to Mountbatten in 1917, the same time that the House of Hanover became the House of Windsor; the later Earl became Lord Louis Mountbatten at that time. He was assigned to his first ship, HMS LION in 1916, shortly after the battle of Jutland. He then transferred to HMS QUEEN ELIZABETH in February 1917, both being consecutive flagships of Admiral David Beatty.

In 1922 he married Edwina Ashley at St. Margaret's Church, Westminster. Born in 1901 and gaining her inheritance in 1921, Edwina was daughter of Colonel W.W. Ashley, PC, MP, later Baron Mount Temple, and Amelia Mary Maud. She was descended from Lord Palmerston and was the granddaughter of Sir Edward Cassel. King Edward VII was her godfather. Edward, Prince of Wales, the future King Edward VIII, was best man at the wedding. Edwina gave Mountbatten a Rolls Royce as a wedding gift, one previously belonging to Edward. The honeymoon was a trip to the U.S., New York City and Hollywood being major stops. Edwina shook hands with Babe Ruth at a game in the former. In the latter, they met Cecil B. De Mille, Charlie

Chaplin, Mary Pickford, and became close friends with Mr. and Mrs. Douglas Fairbanks, Jr.

As World War II began he was commanding officer of the destroyer HMS KELLY which was sunk in the Mediterranean, 23 May 1941. Prime Minister Winston Churchill appointed him Chief of Combined Operations succeeding Lord Roger Keyes. He directed the controversial Dieppe raid, 19 August 1942, in which there were 3000 casualties, mostly Canadians. Winston Churchill continued to advance his career. He was in attendance at several summit conferences, for example, Casablanca, Quebec, Cairo, and Potsdam. At the Quebec conference he was made Supreme Allied Commander, Southeast Asia Command (1943-1946). He was the last Viceroy and Governor-General of India (1946-1948) prior to and during the independence process there. Much interest and controversy has been focused on these crucial offices and events associated with them.

During 1955-1959 he served as First Sea Lord of the Admiralty, a post his father had held, and 1959-1965, as the first Chief of Staff of the Defence Forces, professional head of an innovative combination of the armed forces of Great Britain, a post he held for six years. He opposed British intervention in the Suez crisis of 1956, opposed the British independent nuclear deterrent but, nevertheless, used his influence to facilitate British access to the American nuclear warship propulsion and Polaris nuclear missile programs. He was companion to future monarchs, Edward VIII and George VI, as a young man and later served as mentor to Prince Philip, consort to Queen Elizabeth, and to Prince Charles, heir to the British throne.

Lady Mountbatten died in 1960. Earl Mountbatten was assassinated when an Irish Republican Army bomb blew up his yacht on 27 August 1979 in the Republic of Ireland. There were two daughters, born in 1924 and 1929, and ten grandchildren at the time of his death. The elder daughter, Particia inherited the title, Countess Mountbatten of Burma.

2

Manuscript and Archival Resources

Primary sources for Mountbatten include the Mountbatten Papers, Broadlands Archives, the Royal Archives at Windsor, the PREM series designation at the Public Record Office, minutes of the Chiefs of Staff, minutes of the India Committee of the Cabinet, and various Official Histories of World War II.

BROADLANDS AND OTHER ARCHIVES

For the researcher on Earl Mountbatten and on Lady Mountbatten as well, the first place to go would be the Broadlands Archives, since 1988 located in the Hartley Library of the University of Southampton, Southampton, on the south coast of England. "Sources for Research" [371] and "Broadlands Archives" [44] described the holdings, instructed on the procedures to gain access, and presented addresses, phone numbers, and E-mail access (address: The Hartley Library, University of Southampton, Highfield, Southampton SO9 5NH, Great Britain). The Broadlands Archives continue to be controlled by a committee of Trustees. They were responsible for the selection, first of C.S. Forester [132], and, then, upon his death, Philip Ziegler [445], to be the official biographer of Mountbatten. That is described in detail in the next chapter.

"Broadlands Archives" [44] is a temporary guide to the holdings, a loose-leaf notebook format. The papers of Earl Mountbatten, Lady Mountbatten, Prince Louis of Battenberg, W.W. Ashley, and Sir Edward Cassel were included. The extensive collection of published books in the Mountbatten personal library were described, including books with forewords by Earl Mountbattten and the official histories of World War II.

More permanent guides and a summary catalogue of the papers of Mountbatten were by Christopher Woolgar [437] and L.M. Mitchell [273] respectively. Woolgar described in over 200 pages the Archive and Manuscript Collections held at the Hartley Library at the University of Southampton. The

Special Collections consisted of one and a half miles of shelves, most acquired since 1983, notably, the Wellington, Palmerston, and Mountbatten papers. There was also a significant archive about Jews in Great Britain. Papers of three prominent professors were included: J.S. Bromley, J.M. Roberts, and A. Temple Patterson. The latter [322] wrote the centenary history (1862-1962) of the university. The Broadlands Archives contain materials dating from 1392 to 1979 in six groups. Pertinent were the Mountbatten family papers, 250,000 papers and 50,000 photos. Several sets of papers remain closed: the correspondence of over forty years between Earl and Lady Mountbatten and the correspondence of 1947-1960, hundreds of letters exchanged between Lady Mountbatten and Nehru, leader of India. Also included in that group were the papers of J. Hughes-Hallet, a commander of the Dieppe operation.

The Summary Catalogue by Mitchell [273] was an Occasional Paper of the Library, over 300 pages, describing the Mountbatten papers. Ziegler [445], the official biographer, used these papers extensively, as did Janet Morgan [280], the authoritative biographer of Lady Mountbatten. There was increasing coverage after 1943. The career of Mountbatten was recounted and the pertinent papers held related to each period were described, for example, SAC SEAC, Viceroy, Governor-General, Fourth Sea Lord, First Sea Lord, and Chief of the Defence Staff. There was a section of "Civilian Life" which included charities, organizations, the Broadlands estate, the TV series, speeches, and miscellaneous. The papers of Lady Mountbatten were described. Time Only to Look Forward was a book of published speeches presented by Mountbatten [296], almost 300 pages. They were published in chronological order of presentation.

In addition at the University of Southampton, attached to the Department of Politics, is the Mountbatten Centre for International Studies (address: Highfield, Southampton SO9 5NH), an academic research and policy center.

After the various collections at the Hartley Library in Southampton, the second most productive resource center for the study of Mountbatten is the Public Record Office, the equivalent of the national archives of Great Britain. All pertinent materials which might be associated with Mountbatten are located at Kew on the Thames near Richmond. A guide to the very extensive holdings of official papers of all departments and ministries of the British government was by M.S. Giuseppi [143], three volumes. Louis Atherton [15] has published a guide to the newly released records of the important SOE, held at the Public Record Office, Ruskin Ave., Kew, Richmond, Surrey TW9 4DU, United Kingdom. For the period of his service in India, the late 1940s, official papers and documents can be found at the India Office Library and Records. A British Library publication by Martin Moir [274] describing pertinent holdings is found at India Office Library and Records, Orbit House, 197 Blackfriars Road, London SE1 9NG, United Kingdom.

The British Library, London (formerly, the British Museum Library), Great Russell Street, London WC1B 3DG, United Kingdom, is the equivalent of the Library of Congress where virtually every printed publication can be obtained.

Some important repositories are in the process of change: modern records of the British government were transferred from the old Public Record Office off Fleet Steet to the new facility at Kew during the 1980s; the British Library moved from its former home in the British Museum Reading Room to its own facility several blocks to the north; in late 1997, the National Archives, repository of all official publications of the U.S. government, is reorganizing in a move to a major new facility called Archives II on the campus of the University of Maryland, College Park; and the German Archives Center for Military History will be moving from Freiburg to Potsdam.

The Imperial War Museum, Lambeth Road, London SE1 6HZ, United Kingdom, is a large museum dealing exclusively with the twentieth century, much of it devoted to exhibitions about World War II, a center for researchers, and a large collection of documents, private papers, oral history, photos, and posters. Since 1987 the institution has published an annual journal, The Imperial War Museum Review.

The Churchill Archives, Churchill College, Cambridge University, Cambridge CB3 0DS, United Kingdom, is a relatively new and expanding center for researchers located within the college complex at Churchill College, Cambridge Univeristy.

The Royal Archives, Windsor Castle, Windson, Berkshire SL4 1NJ, United Kingdom, is the official repository for the Crown and its history. Mountbatten figured prominently in the royal family during his lifetime.

Once there were separate armed forces libraries but they have now been combined, another change, into one: The Ministry of Defence Headquarters Libraries, Great Scotland Yard, London SW1A 2HW, United Kingdom. The Royal United Services Institute for Defence Studies, Whitehall Yard, London, SW1A 2ET, United Kingdom, with slight variation in name, has functioned as a center for research, a library, and a sponsor of lectures, publications, and a journal concerned with the armed forces since 1831. It is located in Whitehall Yard, near Parliament Square, Westminster, in London. Mountbatten spoke there on occasion.

Australian War Memorial, GPO Box 345, Canberra, ACT 2601, Australia, is a unique and monumental structure, a combined war memorial, museum, archive, library, and research center. Large collections of battlefield artifacts, artistic depictions of war, and oral history transcriptions are included. There is even a Hall of Memory, a kind of religious chapel.

DIARIES, PAPERS, MEMOIRS, AND OFFICIAL HISTORIES

Mountbatten maintained a diary periodically. Three different sets of the personal diaries of Mountbatten [442, 443, 447], all edited by Philip Ziegler, were published: in chronolgical order, the tour diaries when Mountbatten accompanied Edward, Prince of Wales on world tours in 1921-1922; the diary of Mountbatten when he was SAC SEAC; and From Shore to Shore, his diaries, mostly when he was traveling from 1953-1979. The latter included accounts of subsequent visits to India, Burma, Australia, New Zealand, the White House in Washington, DC, with Admiral Rickover in New London, CT when he sailed on USS SKIPJACK, an American nuclear powered submarine; and periodic cruises on the royal yacht BRITANNIA.

A number of sets of papers of persons closely associated with Mountbatten have been published or are available to researchers. Paul Halpern [150], the prolific naval historian of the period of World War I, edited the extensive papers of Roger Keyes (Admiral of the Fleet Baron of Keyes of Zeebrugge), Chief of Combined Operations whom Mountbatten succeeded in 1941. Keyes [207] himself had published some of his papers dealing with the period 1910-1918.

Two important sets of papers of General Joseph Stilwell [382], Deputy SAC SEAC, among other offices, were published. The most extensive, five volumes, the Stilwell file from the C-B-I theater, was edited by Charles Romanus [351]. Most of the venom of Stilwell was directed at Chiang Kai-shek, but he was a notorious anglophobe and dubbed Mountbatten "Glamor Boy."

Speaking of obstreperous subordinates, the papers of Admiral of the Fleet Sir James Somerville were edited by Michael Simpson [364]. Somerville, naval chief of staff of SEAC, and Mountbatten disagreed about the type of command structure for C-B-I, Mountbatten favoring the MacArthur model, i.e., more centralized control and a personal staff, while Somerville favored the Eisenhower model, a separate, more democratic staff structure. Mountbatten had Somerville recalled. The papers of General Sir Douglas Gracey [147], the British commander sent into Indochina, to Saigon, immediately after the war ended to restore order, were available at the Liddell Hart Centre, King's College, London. Gracey exceeded orders and facilitated the early return of the French colonial administration to Vietnam.

A self-proclaimed intimate and biographer of Mountbatten recently published his memoirs. Richard Hough [181], born in 1922 and author of several naval works and semi-official historian of the Mountbatten family, claimed publication of 95 works. Mountbatten gave Hough [179] access to the Broadlands Archives to research the family history in the early 1970s. Other Days Around Me described voyages on the royal yacht BRITANNIA with Prince Philip and Mountbatten and a tour with Mountbatten of Schloss Heiligenbert near Darmstadt, Germany, the boyhood home. Hough [178, 180] claimed he proposed an interim official biography, but the family objected. After the assassination, he proceeded to complete a biography: "It's what Mountbatten would have wanted." It came out a year after the assassination. "It went straight to the top of the bestseller list. . . . serial rights were 50,000 pounds more. . . . and the biography of Edwina did pretty well too." Hough made frequent observations about the personal life of Mountbatten including some psychological speculations. Mountbatten and Barbara Cartland, a close friend to Lady Mountbatten before her death, were "almost lovers. . . . but not bed"; he was not homosexual, his sexual drive "taking third place to his ambition and achievement of excellence"; and he felt insecure about his intellectual abilities: "the more humble and less educated people tended to admire him greatly while the higher up the social scale the more marked were the reservations." Candidness persisted in observations about Lady Mountbatten: yes, she had affairs, but "not Paul Robeson" (pp. 216-225).

A short memoir and quasi-obituary of Mountbatten was published in early 1980 in Naval Institute Proceedings, written by Prince Philip [325], husband of Queen Elizabeth II and protege of Mountbatten. It was profusely illustrated. Prince Philip noted his service of 52 years in the Royal Navy. He had specialized in signals, wireless, and electronics.

The Mountbattens, especially Earl Mountbatten, sought out celebrities, on their honeymoon in the U.S. and during the war years. They were frequently in company with movie stars and famous authors. Mountbatten personally facilitated film projects and the famous TV documentary on his life, made in the 1960s. For example, the relationship with Sir Noel Coward led to the movie "In Which We Serve" [192], one of the most successful of the 1940s. The diaries and autobiography of Coward [85, 86] have been published. Mountbatten also sought out Evelyn Waugh who was an officer during the war. The diaries of Waugh, edited by Michael Davie [94], have been published.

Two close personal friends of both of the Mountbattens have produced recollections about their relationships. In three works, two recent, the American film star Douglas Fairbanks, Jr. [119, 120, 121], fondly remembered and praised Earl and Lady Mountbaten: in a family photo album containing several pictures; in The Salad Days, a memoir with many citations about "Dickie," Edwina, and daughter Particia; and A Hell of a War, a sequel which was dedicated to the memory of Mountbatten, "hero and friend and honorary God-father of my three Graces, Daphne, Victoria, and Melissa" (introductory section). Fairbanks served in the USN and spent some time in London during the war, actually assigned to the staff of COHQ during the planning for the Dieppe operation. A close friend to Lady Mountbatten who remained a friend to Mountbatten after 1960 was the prolific novelist, Barbara Cartland [62]. In a note in Love at the Helm, she observed that Mountbatten frequently assisted her with historical background of many of her novels, especially the naval ones. Cartland contributed the proceeds of several novels, first to Lady Mountbatten's charity, the St. John Ambulance

Brigade, and a later one, immediately after the death of Mountbatten, to the Mountbatten Memorial Trust.

The Autobiography of Solly Zuckerman [449], two volumes, presented the personal experiences of this noted scientific advisor and arms negotiator who worked closely with Mountbatten, for example, at COHQ.   Brian Bond [38] edited the diaries of General Sir Henry Pownall, Chief of Staff to Mountbatte at SEAC. It was enlightening on Mountbatten, Orde Wingate, and others. There were also references to Mountbatten in the diaries of Robert Bruce Lockhart, edited by Kenneth Young [440].

Robin Higham [168, 169], to whom the China-Burma-India volume was dedicated, is the original historian of the phenomenon of official histories. Official Histories began with a series of explanatory essays about official histories followed by 600 pages allocated to individual case studies by country. The critique that official histories can be manipulated and censored is faced and rationalized. In an essay, Stephen Roskill [356], the official British naval historian of the war, pointed out how different his history was compared to the six-volume work of Winston Churchill. Roskill gained access to all sources and was free to include what he believed appropriate. He recalled the previous case where Julian Corbett was censored by Admiralty authorities when writing the official naval history of World War I. The pertinent volume associated with the theater under Mountbatten was S.W. Kirby [210], The War against Japan, five volumes. This was the official history which condemned Orde Wingate and the CHINDITS, a topic reviewed below in the chapter on the Southeast Asian Command. Mountbatten and Churchill have been accused of manipulating the British official histories.

Of the British Dominions, Australia, Canada, and the colony India played important roles within C-B-I.   Canada and its contributions were applicable to some controversy related to Mountbatten. W.A.B. Douglas [104] wrote a summary overview of the role of Canada and C.P. Stacey [377] wrote the official Canadian Army history.

BIBLIOGRAPHIES

Comparatively little assistance to the researcher on World War II or the Asian/Pacific war in the matter of locating manuscripts and manuscript collections currently exists. Some assistance is forthcoming with the publication of Loyd Lee [226], Handbook of the Literature and Research of World War II. The first volume covers the European/Atlantic war; the entire second volume is devoted to the Asian/Pacific war. It will provide broad and comprehensive assistance.

As previously noted, the Asian/Pacific war can be subdivided into three geographic theaters, the Southwest Pacific under the command of General

MacArthur, the Central Pacific under the command of Admiral Nimitz, and China-Burma-India, ultimately commanded by Earl Mountbatten.   James Controvich [77], The Central Pacific Campaign, briefly annotated 1130 items in the Bibliographies of Battles and Leaders series. The contribution of Controvich focused on the middle years of the campaign, 1943-1944.   Three additional volumes in the series require review.   The others, as with the volume at hand, are historiographical surveys and annotated bibliographies, recently published or forthcoming by Eugene Rasor [339, 340, 341] of Emory and Henry College: General Douglas MacArthur, 760 entries, published in 1994, The Southwest Pacific Campaign, 1535 entries, published in 1996, The Solomons Islands Campaign, 544 entries, published in 1997, and China-Burma-India, forthcoming. Unfortunately, there is no equivalent bibliography for Admiral Nimitz, partly because of comparatively less attention devoted to him in published works.

There is a chapter below on Mountbatten and the Royal Navy of Great Britain. For it, there is a general and a specific bibliography: Eugene Rasor [338], British Naval History since 1815, and Derek Law [223], The Royal Navy in World War II.   Both Rasor and Law presented extensive annotation of over 3000 and almost 2000 entries, respectively.

More general assistance can be found in Robin Higham [167] Guide to the Sources of British Military History which covered Great Britain and consisted of 25 historiographical essays by prominent experts for chronological periods or special topics. Each essay incorporated critical analyses of at least a hundred of the most important sources. The British guide has been updated with a single, extensive supplement (1251 pages), edited by Gerald Jordan [200] of York University in Canada.   6400 entries are incorporated in it alone.   There is a bibliographical guide for Mahatma Gandhi by April Carter [60] in the Bibliographies of World Leaders series.

3

Biographical Works about Earl Mountbatten and Lady Mountbatten

The personal life and times of Earl Mountbatten and Lady Mountbatten have attracted significant interest. He was the obvious important interest with a dozen published, but she, in her own right, was the subject of half a dozen serious biographies. Quality varied. As is the case throughout this historiographical narrative section, the best are reviewed first with lesser lights appearing at the end.

EARL MOUNTBATTEN

C.S. Forester [132] was originally selected to write the official biography of Mountbatten. A biography of the famous naval fiction and history writer, author of the ten Hornblower adventure novels, was by Sanford Sternlicht [381]. After the death of Forester in 1966 Philip Ziegler [445] was contracted to complete the biography. That was published amid much favorable comment in 1985. Ziegler had unrestricted access to the Broadlands Archives. The official biography was a comprehensive, candid appraisal of all: vanity, ambition, successes, failures, snobbery, action for social justice, living in "the fast lane," marital problems of Earl and Lady Mountbatten, loyalty, and continuing extraordinary use of power and influence. It has been described as "appallingly frank" (R.A. Callahan in Choice) which "demythologizes but does not debunk" (Gerald Jordan in Military Affairs) Earl Mountbatten. It was divided into five sections, covering roughly a decade each, a total of 52 chapters. Three of the five parts were devoted to the naval career. In his review of Mountbatten in Mariner's Mirror, Eric Grove of the University of Hull, called Mountbatten "perhaps the most remarkable naval officer of the twentieth century." Ziegler observed that Attlee's choice of Mountbatten as Viceroy and Nehru's choice of him as Governor-Gerneral were both "inspired." There were 50 pages of reference notes and a six-page bibliographical essay. Several reviewers praised it as a model official biography. Ziegler [446] presented the

British Studies Distinguished Lecture at the University of Texas, the title: "Mountbatten Revisited."

The title of the Hough [180] biography was <u>Mountbatten: Hero of Our Time</u>, as noted above, published on the first anniversary of the assassination and dedicated "To his memory." Called an "informal study," he did admit it was not sanctioned by the family, indeed, the family objected to its publication. He had access to the Broadlands Archives for the Mountbatten family history [179] but not for the biography of Mountbatten or Lady Mountbatten [178]. <u>Mountbatten</u> opened with the assassination and proceeded with a chronological account of the life before the spectacular death.

Another biography, <u>The Life and Times of Lord Mountbatten</u> with a foreword by Mountbatten and an additional French edition, was by John Terraine [396, 397]. It too was not authorized but was the basis for the TV documentary narrated by Mountbatten [237]. Originally written in 1968, a postscript was added to the edition of 1980 (pp. 196-97), recounting the assassination. There were several other IRA bombings on the same day. Mountbatten lamented two errors: the Burma transfer of power imbroglio and not pursuing his opposition to the Suez affair.

The most recent biography, <u>Mountbatten: The Private Story</u>, was by Brian Hoey [172], who insisted it was a look at the private Mountbatten, a portrait of his character, "his troubled marriage, his love affairs, his attitude toward money, and his fascination with things royal." Many interviews were conducted with those who knew him best: his two daughters, his "mistress," Prince Philip, Ziegler, Woolgar, and Douglas Fairbanks, Jr. The Broadlands Archives at the University of Southampton were used. Every fact has been verified, but it was not reassuring to add "For this reason I have not included footnotes" (p. vii-ix). It is poorly organized and hard to follow. Mountbatten was not bisexual or homosexual, as rumored. The affair between Lady Mountbatten and Nehru did occur. An entire chapter was devoted to his financial situation. Mountbatten began planning the most minute details of his funeral in the late 1960s. The body lay in state first at Romsey Abbey, then at St. James Palace (a total of 75,000 viewed it), then to Westminster Abbey, and then a cortege to Waterloo Station where a special train proceeded to Romsey Abbey. Mountbatten had even described the menu for lunch on the train. There was much ceremony, but it was not a state funeral. International, military-naval, royal family, and representatives of dozens of organizations all had specified places.

Another recent biographical entry on Mountbatten, <u>The Princely Sailor</u>, was by Sir Ian McGeoch [248], a British admiral and 40-year veteran. The accomplishments, especially a unified defence organization and independence for India and Pakistan, outweighed the faults. A kind of "quasi-biography" was in the popular paperback series, <u>Ballantine Illustrated History of World War II: War Leader</u>, by Arthur Swinson [389], including numerous black and white photos. Swinson died in 1971. Barrie Pitt wrote the introduction: "Mountbatten is a phenomenon--judged by any standard in any age" (pp. 6-7). The entire career of Mountbatten was affected by the humiliating resignation of Prince Louis Battenberg, accused of being pro-German at the beginning of World War I. Most of this book was devoted to events of World War II, the Dieppe raid and SAC SEAC. Service in India was the focus of Ray L. Murphy [305], Last Viceroy: The Life and Times of Rear Admiral the Earl Mountbatten of Burma. He moved from the "Phoenix Command" to "Pro-consul of Compromise."

A short study, Mountbatten of Burma, was by George E. Baker [19], biographer of King Charles II. A biography for juveniles, The Supremo: Lord Louis Mountbatten and the Testing of Democracy, was by Irving Werstein [418], who died in 1971. Mountbatten was sailor, soldier, statesman, investor, and educator. Mountbatten compared the treatment of his father to that of Alfred Dreyfus.

The comprehensive thirteen-part TV documentary, "The Life and Times of Lord Mountbatten" [237] will be reviewed below.

Various levels of holders of staff positions, personal and official, and a "novel" have also appeared. A butler of fifty years, Charles Smith [366], wrote a memoir. Born in 1908, Smith began service in 1930 and was recalled for aid at the time of the assassination. The valet of Mountbatten of ten years, William Evans [118], wrote recollections, listing all of his honors and titles and claiming active membership in over 200 organizations. John Barratt [28], the private secretary wrote about the private lives With the Greatest Respect. The Press Attache while Mountbatten was in India, Alan Campbell-Johnson [56], wrote Mission with Mountbatten. He kept a diary and was the first to provide details on high level negotiations behind closed doors related to the transfer of power. Admiral of the Fleet: The Life of Sir Charles Lambe by Oliver Warner [414], with the introduction by Mountbatten, was a biography of a friend and prominent colleague who became First Sea Lord after Mountbatten. Finally, there was the curious "novel," Lord Mountbatten: The Last Viceroy, by David Butler [52]. It was the basis for a TV series depicting the transfer of power in India produced by George Walker with Nicol Williamson as Mountbatten.

The Mountbattens cultivated close relations with celebrities and the biographies of some of them note friendships and common causes with the Mountbattens. Two examples were Sir Noel Coward and Evelyn Waugh. Biographies of Coward abound and include those by Graham Payn [324], Philip Hoare [171], Clive Fisher [127], Charles Castle [65], two by Cole Lesley [229, 230], and an account of the literary and media accomplishments of Coward, especially "In Which We Serve," which Coward produced, directed, and starred in the Mountbatten role, and which received a special Academy Award. The biography of Evelyn Waugh was by Martin Stannard [378], two volumes.

There are the standard entries and essays in traditional biographical dictionaries. Most detailed was the comprehensive biographical essay in the

Dictionary of National Biography, 1971-1980, the eighth supplement [98, 300], a ten-page, double column entry written by the official biographer, Philip Ziegler. Family background, education, early naval service, the world tours, HMS KELLY, COHQ, SAC SEAC, Viceroy and Governor-General, and senior naval officer were all reviewed. Problems facing Mountbatten upon arrival in SEAC were "monsoon, malaria, and morale." Both Admiral A.B. Cunningham and Winston Churchill objected to Mountbatten being appointed First Sea Lord in 1954, both holding out and finally reluctantly being persuaded. Mountbatten drafted a letter of resignation in August 1956, objecting to plans for the Suez operation, but was disuaded from submitting it. Lord Beaverbrook, the powerful press lord and government minister, was once a supporter of Mountbatten but shifted to persistent critic at about the time of the Dieppe raid. His biography, and the sometime director of the Beaverbook library, was by A.J.P. Taylor [394].

Entries in Who's Who, 1978-1979: Annual Biographical Dictionary and Who Was Who, 1971-1980, vol. VIII [301, 302], were similar: long lists of titles, honors, organizations, and some career highlights. Field Marshal Lord Michael Carver [63, 64] was editor of two compilations which included essays on or about Mountbatten: Twentieth-Century Warriors and The War Lords. In the former Mountbatten was credited with preparation from as early as 1941 for integration, cooperation, and coordination of the armed forces, from COHQ to CDS. The pay-off was the Falklands/Malvinas campaign of 1982. Carver himself served as CDS after Mountbatten. In the latter there was a complete biographical essay (pp. 357-74) by Ronald Brockman. Only three of the 43 essays were from the Royal Navy. Mountbatten was included among the 3000 entries in The Harper Enclcyclopedia of Military Biography: From 3500 to the Present, a reference encyclopedia, the 4th edition, 1993, 200 to 1000 word essays, "Caesar to Schwarzkopf." The editor was Trevor Dupuy [108] and the pertinent essay (pp. 527-28) was by David Bongard. John Canning [59] edited 100 Great Modern Lives: Makers of the World Today from Faraday to Kennedy. Mountbatten rated an essay (pp. 594-99), written by Ian Fellowes-Gordon.

In the 1960s Kenneth Harris [158] collected nineteen interviews, many of them for the BBC. One was with Mountbatten (pp. 138-59) and it focused on memories of the war. He recalled that when he was recalled from the U.S. in 1941 where he was to take command of HMS ILLUSTRIOUS, an aircraft carrier undergoing repairs in Newport News, Virginia, he was upset and reluctant to give up the opportunity, but Churchill insisted that he take over at COHQ. There, he claimed, he influenced developments of landing craft and eventually the great Mulberry artificial harbor complex.

LADY EDWINA MOUNTBATTEN

Clearly, coverage of Earl Mountbatten has been extensive and wide ranging. So has that of Lady Mountbatten, although less general. Patricia, Countess Mountbatten of Burma and Lady Pamela Hicks, the two daughters, asked Janet Morgan [280], biographer of Agatha Christie and editor of the Richard Crossman diaries, to write the sanctioned biography. She was given access to the Broadlands Archives. It is too detailed, the author is too familiar-- first names are used throughout--it is too long, and there are no scholarly supplements, only a scanty index. It was the story of the God-daughter of King Edward VII for whom the Edwardian age was named. She was an indulged millionairess who transformed herself to a hard-working, devoted campaigner for health care and public causes, dying on the Pacific island of Borneo while conducting an inspection tour for St. John Ambulance Brigade Overseas. There were accounts of the infidelities of both, his French mistress, Yola Letellier, and one of her lovers, Bunny Phillips. Another was Nehru. There was serious talk of divorce about 1950 but he convinced her to abandon that.

Inevitably, Richard Hough [178] got into the act. The blurb of this popular biography described her as of "the Prince of Wale's set, . . . the richest woman in the land, . . . a privileged semi-royal and socialist anti-monarchist, . . . the object of widespread scrutiny and controversy." She was a radical in her social philosophy and a humanitarian activist: specific interventions in the cases of Jews under Hitler, the suffering and homeless, Allied POWs, victims of communal violence in India, and roving ambassador for St. John Ambulance Brigade.

Earl Mountbatten wrote the foreword for the biography, Edwina, by Madeline Masson [263], published in three editions between 1958 and 1975. The portrait on the cover was by Salvador Dali, the original hanging at Broadlands. Mountbatten noted in the 1975 edition that the family received 6000 telegrams and letters after her death. He was descended from Charlemagne, she from Kings Edward IV and Henry VII of the fifteenth century. Dennis Holman [174] published a short biography in 1952. Immediately after her death, Marjorie M Pratt, Countess of Brecknoch [334] published Edwina Mountbatten: Her Life in Pictures, another short, popular biography. The foreword was by Sir Arthur Bryant. It described a "brilliant and happy marriage" (p. 3). Many family pictures supported the narrative.

The Dictionary of National Biography entry on Lady Mountbatten [98, 297] was in the 1951-1960 edition, the biographical essay of two pages, double columns was by Alan Campbell-Johnson, press attache for the Mountbattens in India. Her fortune came from her grandfather, Sir Ernest Cassel who died in 1921. Her role in the liberation of thousands of Allied Prisoners of War of the Japanese at the end of the war was praised. A short entry was printed in Who Was Who, 1951-1960 [298], listing facts of her education and honors.

4

Works about Mountbatten and the Royal Family

The first place to search for British dynastic and aristocratic genealogy is Burke's Guide to the Royal Family [51]. It is in the Burke's Genealogical series and, inevitably, the foreword of the 1973 edition was by Earl Mountbatten. He recalled six reigns in his own lifetime. Queen Victoria had held him at his christening. The royal family had abandoned all German styles and titles in 1917 and took "Windsor" as the dynastic name, at the same time that Battenberg was changed to Mountbatten.

On a broader front D.C.B. Lieven [236] wrote The Aristocracy of Europe, 1815-1914, containing details of the extensive and elaborate relationships of the noble and royal genealogy of Europe in the crucial nineteenth century. There was discussion of their wealth, life, manners, and morals, and roles in war and politics. Crowned Cousins: The Anglo-German Royal Connection by Alan Palmer [316] followed the descendants of Frederick, the Elector of Palatine and Elizabeth, daughter of King James I, who married in 1612. This established the Hanoverian connection.

Specifically for Great Britain, Theo Aronson [13] recently wrote The Royal Family at War, mostly hagiography about King George VI and Elizabeth II. Mountbatten was a second cousin and never played a role of wartime representative of the monarchy, much as he may have desired that personally. For example, George VI wanted to visit India during the war but Churchill forbade it. There was special sensitivity that such monarchical displays might exaggerate American fears of European colonialism. Mountbatten actually urged the king to visit India. The last king-emperor was destined never to set foot in India. Similarly, John Winton [431], again excluding Mountbatten, wrote Captains and Kings: The Royal Family and the Royal Navy, 1901-1981. George V, George VI, Edward VIII, Prince Philip, Prince Charles, and Prince Andrew and their naval connections were reviewed. However, Cecil Hampshire [155] in Royal Sailors included Mountbatten when reviewing British princes and dukes in the Royal Navy since the seventeenth century. Famous naval kings were

James II and William IV and royal relatives included Prince Louis of Battenberg, serving 46 years, and Mountbatten, 52 years. The brother of George VI, the Duke of Kent, was killed in World War II. Prince Philip, Prince Charles, and Prince Andrew all served significantly in the Royal Navy.

Several studies were collective biographies of the Battenbergs-Mountbattens. There was a German edition of From Battenberg to Mountbatten by E.H. Cookridge [78, 79]. The operative name was Hesse, the dynastic name of a series of Grand Dukes going back to Charlemagne. In 1851 the name Battenberg was created, changed to Mountbatten in 1917 under pressure from anti-German elements. Mountbatten [289] himself wrote The Mountbatten Lineage: The Direct Descent of the Family of Mountbatten from the House of Brabant and the Rulers of Hesse, originally in 1946, revived in 1958, and "Prepared for private circulation." He traced back 44 generations. "Brabant/Hessian/Mountbatten" can be traced back to the fourth century, to Clovis and Pippin. In it he expressed the hope Queen Elizabeth would assume the family name of Mountbatten. That was thwarted by Queen Mary and then Elizabeth herself. A similar, simple, and straightforward effort was by Cyril Hankins [156], also privately published.

The journalist, Douglas Liversidge [238], wrote The Mountbattens: From Battenberg to Windsor, published in 1978. Mountbatten was obviously upset, especially with the provocative subtitle. In the copy in the Mountbatten library, "The author never made contact with any of the family" was written inside the cover.

Philip Ziegler recommended Richard Hough [179], Louis and Victoria: The Family History of the Mountbattens, the product of the request by Mountbatten to Hough to research in the Broadlands Archives and elsewhere and write a history of the family. It was published in 1974, and updated in 1984 after the assassination. More recently, Antony Lambton [219] published The Mountbattens and promised a second volume. The first covered up to "the young Mountbatten."

Admiral Mark Kerr [205] wrote a biography of the father of Mountbatten, Prince Louis of Battenberg, later Marquis of Milford Haven (1854-1921), published in 1934. The resignation of October 1914 was fully covered (pp. 246-81). A few senior officers, mostly retired, resorted to "lowdown tactics" and "contemptible gossips," forcing the resignation. Lord Beresford was mentioned elsewhere.

Two works, by Brian Connell [75] and Alden Hatch [161] presented several biographical case studies of these same personalities. Both included Prince Louis, Lord Louis, and Prince Philip. Connell added Sir Ernest Cassel and Lady Mountbatten. Hatch used the subtitle, The Last Royal Success Story. A daughter of Prince Louis and Victoria Battenberg was Louise Mountbatten who married the Crown Prince of Sweden, subsequently becoming Queen. She died in 1965. Her biography was by Margit Fjellman [128].

The Mountbattens were cousins of the Windsors. An actual effort by Mountbatten to have the Windsor dynastic name changed to Mountbatten was described by Roland Flamini [129] in Sovereign (pp. 245-48). Prince Philip was supportive because he desired that his children bear his name. There were many references to "Dickie." David Cannadine [58], a noted authority on the history of England and the monarchy, collected 30 book reviews he wrote in the 1980s, many of them about monarchy, in The Pleasures of the Past. Victoria and Albert, the latter definitely not comparable to Thomas Jefferson--Albert had designed Osborne House and Jefferson, Monticello--George V, a political zero, Edward VIII, a selfish simpleton who made his own choice and never ceased to regret it, and Mountbatten, the first of many other morticians of Empire, were included. "The Windsors: A Royal Family" [430] a TV documentary, a British-American production, four-hours, was shown in 1994. It was the last great dynasty of Europe. Wags called it "twits and twerps."

Deteriorating into muckraking was Donald Spoto [374], The Decline and Fall of the House of Windsor, a recent addition, focusing on royal scandals and media stars. Another superficial effort was Charles Higham [166], Elizabeth and Philip. He was author of biographies of movie stars. The matter of the Mountbatten surname was reviewed. Rumors of sexual eccentricities, sadomasochism, and worse concerning Mountbatten were aired. While Richard Hough [177] was researching and writing about the Mountbattens, he wrote a book on the young Windsors, the six children of King George V and Queen Mary. The cousin, Mountbatten, figured prominently.

More scholarly biographies of these monarchs have been forthcoming. Kenneth Rose [354] was the biographer of King George V, monarch while Mountbatten was growing up. Philip Ziegler [444], official biographer of Mountbatten, next turned to an official biography of King Edward VIII (1894-1952). The depiction was not flattering. Edward was immature, a heavy drinker, philanderer, masochist, and lazy. The Duchess was a vampire. There was fear at the time of the abdication crisis, in late 1936, that Churchill would be called in as Prime Minister and form a royalist, even a fascist, government. After abdication they were made Duke [429] and Duchess [428] of Windsor. They wrote memoirs, published in the 1950s. John Wheeler-Bennett [420], like Ziegler, gained full access to the royal archives at Windsor, wrote the official biography of the next king, George VI. A more recent biography of George VI which incorporated new evidence about the Duke and Duchess of Windsor was by Sarah Bradford [40]. All contained many references to Mountbatten.

Prince Philip has been an attractive subject for biographers. An older one, 1971, was by Basil Boothroyd [39], a semi-official product. More recently were biographies by Peter Lane [220], Denis Judd [201], John Parker [320], and Tim Heald [162]. All stressed the close ties to Mountbatten, his mentor. All dealt with the controversy about the dynastic name. In 1959, Queen Elizabeth agreed to change the name to Mountbatten-Windsor but no "HRHs" would use that name, continuing to use the title, House of Windsor. Beaverbrook and Churchill entered the fray. Lane devoted several chapters to the name imbroglio. The blurb of the Judd biography described Philip as "the most controversial, unconventional, and misunderstood member of Britain's royal family," this in 1980.

Since that time, Prince Charles may have replaced that description, especially after the expose-type, semi-official biography of Charles by Jonathan Dimbleday [100], published in 1994 by a prominent broadcaster-journalist. Charles blamed Philip and Mountbatten for abusing him and making his life miserable. The royal marriage of 1981 ended in 1996. The affair with Camilla Parker-Bowles was covered.

5

Works about Mountbatten and the Royal Navy

Earl Mountbatten never wavered from the time of the resignation of his father, Prince Louis of Battenberg, from the office of First Sea Lord, the highest office for a professional naval officer in the Royal Navy, in 1914, from the time he himself first went aboard HMS LION in 1916, and throughout the rest of his professional life, from his career commitment to the Royal Navy. It remained his highest priority and, time after time, for example when Churchill recalled him from his newly assigned command of HMS ILLUSTRIOUS in 1941, when he was made Viceroy of India 1947, and when he was made Governor-General of India, also in 1947, he was reluctant to take these positions which he saw as diversions from his ultimate objective to become First Sea Lord and exonerate the humiliation of his father.

The Royal Navy in the twentieth century was a deteriorating force, moving down from the first line of defense, a position it had enjoyed during the height of British imperialism and commercial hegemony, to equal competitor with the Royal Air Force before and during the Second World War, and continued competition and dimunition in the postwar era. Mountbatten played a prominent role in being an advocate for sea power but he also, from as early as the early 1940s, recognized the increasing importance of interservice cooperation and ultimate intergration of all three of the armed forces. He initiated the early moves toward the centralized and integrated structure which led to creation of the Ministry of Defence. He became Chief of the Defence Staff and led in the preparation for creation of the Ministry.

The father of Mountbatten, Prince Louis of Battenberg [299], prepared and presented a lecture, the Rede Lecture of 1918 at Cambridge University, on the history of the Royal Navy in the nineteenth century. A more general survey of naval history, a series of expert essays, was edited by Gerald Jordan [200], Naval Warfare in the Twentieth Century. There was an essay on the Dieppe raid which will be properly reviewed below. Most recently, J.R. Hill [170] edited a folio size luxury-produced history of the Royal Navy, again a series of essays by the most distinguished naval historians.

Mountbatten served in the Royal Navy during the First World War. The best naval history of the war, published in 1994, was by Paul Halpern [151]. There are more choices for naval histories of the Second World War. The best on the Royal Navy, again a recent publication, was Engage the Enemy More Closely, a Nelsonian motto, written by the prominent and provocative twentieth-century British historian, Correlli Barnett [27]. The perspective of the sailors was represented in The War at Sea by John Winton [433], with an introduction by Mountbatten.

Mountbatten attained the highest naval rank, Admiral of the Fleet, was commanding officer of a destroyer and a destroyer flotilla in combat, was Chief, COQH, and ultimately Supreme Allied Commander of one of the most important theaters of the war, yet, he was never considered one of the great naval commanders of the war.   This was demonstrated, for example, in three compilations: Charles Owen [311], No More Heroes: The Royal Navy in the Twentieth Century, Stephen Howarth [183], Men of War: Great Naval Leaders of World War II, and Martin Stephen [380], The Fighting Admirals: British Admirals of the Second World War. Mountbatten was not included in any of these.   A partial explanation can be gleaned from the Owen piece which lamented the vanishing style, the end of the commander elite best represented by St. Vincent and Nelson in the previous century.

More specifically, personal experiences of Mountbatten were covered in two works, a history of the Royal Naval College, Dartmouth by Edward Hughes [186], and Signal!: A History of Signalling in the Royal Navy by Barrie Kent [204].   Mountbatten attended RNC, Dartmouth and attained the highest professional competence during his formative years, the interwar period, in naval communications. In the latter, there was a section on "Mountbatten, the signal officer" (pp. 74-78).

Seen by some as the greatest British naval historian was Arthur Marder, most famous for his milti-volume history of the Royal Navy from about 1880 to 1920. Marder [259] also, later in life and unfinished at his death in 1980, wrote a two-volume history, Old Friends, New Enemies: The Royal Navy and the Imperial Japanese Navy. Marder covered two controversies associated with Mountbatten, in both cases also involving Winston Churchill, notorious for personally intervening in naval matters. In the first case, Mountbatten and Churchill combined to disrupt the career of Sir James Somerville, naval staff deputy in the SEAC command. Marder claimed the ambition of Mountbatten exaggerated matters, leading to the recall of Somerville.   The second case concerned the official British naval history of the war by Stephen Roskill [356], in addition later to write Churchill and the Admirals.   Marder claimed Mountbatten and Churchill manipulated Roskill's official history and further mislead Marder himself.

The most important combat experience of Mountbatten during World War II was in the closely fought naval competition in the Mediterranean Sea as the Germans and Italians expanded in North Africa and then in the Balkan peninsula. The Germans invaded Yugoslavia and Greece in the spring of 1941, overran both. The British decided to oppose the invasion of its ally, Greece, and sent troops and forces to the Balkans. The Germans drove them into the sea, then conducted an airborne invasion of the island of Crete, to which the British had withdrawn. Though quite costly for the Germans, they captured Crete and controlled the sea around it. The British navy carried out a costly rescue and withdrawal operation.

Mountbatten had become commanding officer of HMS KELLY and the 5th Destroyer Flotilla early in the war. KELLY suffered damage in May 1940 off the Denmark coast and was repaired. Then she was ordered to the Mediterranean and was involved in the Crete operations of May 1941, when she was sunk by air attack with a loss of 130 men on 23 May 1941. Mountbatten himself barely survived, abandoning ship at the last and was almost pulled under as KELLY went down. HMS KASHMIR, another destroyer in the squadron, was lost. Survivors from both were picked up by HMS KIPLING, a third destroyer of the squadron, and taken to Alexandria, Egypt.

Interest and writing about HMS KELLY were high. The story of HMS KELLY would be the basis for one of the most popular and effective British war movies, "In Which We Serve" [192] produced, directed, and starring Sir Noel Coward. Kenneth Poolman [331] wrote a "biography," The KELLY: HMS KELLY, the Story of Mountbatten's Warship. Mountbatten wrote the foreword and publication continued into the 1980s. He recalled his naval career and that KELLY was the one ship he remembered in his long career, "the happiest ship" (pp. 5-6). A veteran naval officer and journalist, William Pattinson [323], wrote Mountbatten and the Men of the KELLY, with the foreword by Charles, Prince of Wales and a preface by Philip Ziegler. A feature was the story of the KELLY Reunion Association, an active organization which sponsored a series of memorial reunions. The copy in the Mountbatten library was folio size and signed by 20 or 30 veteran crewmembers. Mountbatten had written over 900 personal letters to the survivors. There is a KELLY Memorial at the Hebburn on Tyne Cemetary. Most recently, Richard Hough [176] wrote Bless Our Ship: Mountbatten and the KELLY, 1991. It was divided into three sections, the man, the ship, and the final battle. Hough interviewed many survivors.

There were three accounts of the battle of Crete, May 1941: Stanley Pack [314] in the Sea Battles in Close-Up series, G.C. Kiriakopoulos [211], Ten Days to Destiny, and David A. Thomas [400], Nazi Victory. Pack noted that the British forces were stretched to the limit and with the retreat, stretched beyond the limit. Three cruisers and eight destroyers were lost by the Royal Navy. The German assault was entirely airborne and losses were also enormous. Mediterranean Maelstrom: HMS JERVIS and the Fourteenth Flotilla by G.G.

Connell [76] was an account of a sister-ship of HMS KELLY and its operations in the Mediterranean, 1940-1943. Of the 16 "J" and "K" class destroyers in the Mediterranean campaign, only four survived.

The exciting and fatal saga of HMS KELLY was the inspiration for the wartime British movie, "In Which We Serve" [192], made in 1942, produced, directed, and starring Sir Noel Coward, also starring John Mills. It was a skillful propaganda and patriotic film at a crucial time for the British, when they were fighting alone and retreating everywhere. Coward was awarded a special Oscar. The context and significance of "In Which We Serve" was presented in Anthony Aldgate [5], Britain Can Take It: The British Cinema in the Second World War, with a recent edition in 1994. Chapter 9 was about the movie (pp. 187-217).

Coward had met the Mountbattens in July 1941 and heard the story of HMS KELLY. Mountbatten assisted in arranging official collaboration of the Royal Navy. There was opposition to Coward because of his notorious lifestyle. Beaverbrook, who disliked Mountbatten and Coward, attempted to obstruct. Coward retaliated by clearly showing a notorious headline, "No War" from a Beaverbrook newspaper.

In an article, Clive Coultass [82] wrote of another naval film project in the 1950s facilitated by Mountbatten, about the famous naval battle of the River Plate, one of the last traditional ship-vs-ship naval battles. It took place early in the war and resulted in the German battleship, GRAF SPEE, being scuttled. Mountbatten also wrote the foreword to a documentary anthology about the battle of the River Plate by Sir Eugene Millington-Drake [272].

Five other books associated with Mountbatten and the Royal Navy deserve mention, Mountbatten writing the forewords of the first four and the ship, the subject of the fifth, was used in a decisive way in the famous COHQ raid on St. Nazaire. Mountbatten wrote forewords for the standard histories of British battleships, by Oscar Parkes [321], and British destroyers, by Edgar March [256]. British Warship Names by Thomas Manning [254] was a hefty tome containing comprehensive information about all warships of the Royal Navy, when, what, and major operations. The Ship Names Committee was described. John Winton [432], the prolific naval historian, wrote Sink the HAGURO!: The Last Destroyer Action of the Second World War, about five British destroyers sinking a large Japanese cruiser in the Malacca Straits, 15 May 1945. The destroyer CAMPBELTOWN by Al Ross [357] was about the ex-USS BUCHANAN, one of the 50 destroyers-for-bases warships which was used by COHQ as the target ship with explosives which successfully destroyed the entrance to the large drydock at St. Nazaire, the primary objective of the raid.

E.F. Gueritz [149] in an article, "Nelson's Blood," recalled many of the strong traditions in the history of the Royal Navy: the rum ration, Nelson's Band of Brothers, courageous exploits such as those at the River Plate, sinking of the BISMARCK, and defense of convoys. Mountbatten was seen as a "newcomer" and "outsider," not in the tradition and not fully accepted in the "band of brothers."

6

Works about Mountbatten and World War II

Earl Mountbatten, of course, remained in the Royal Navy throughout the Second World War even though he also attained flag ranks in the Army and Air Force, and was later Viceroy and Governor-General of India. He would return to his naval career, reverting to the rank of Rear Admiral, in 1948. After the loss of HMS KELLY and his return home, he was ordered to the U.S. to take command of the aircraft carrier, HMS ILLUSTRIOUS, undergoing repair in Newport News, Virginia. He looked forward to taking command of a major combatant ship, but it was not to be. Enroute, he stopped by Washington and met American naval officials. Late in 1941 he received orders from Winston Churchill to return to England and join the staff of Combined Operations, then under the direction of Lord Roger Keyes, a naval hero of World War I.

COMBINED OPERATIONS

In his noted study, Churchill as Warlord, Ronald Lewin [232] began with Churchill becoming Prime Minister and War Minister in May 1940. He described Churchill as energetic, pugnacious, egocentric, emotional, an egomaniac, and courageous. He constantly produced initiatives and demanded action, in the case of the war against Germany, offensive initiatives. That would inevitably entail amphibious and other special operations and maximum cooperation and coordination of the three armed services, what Churchill would dub Combined Operations. In July 1940 the Combined Operations Headquarters (COHQ) was created with Admiral Lord Roger Keyes as Director.

There is a London dissertation, "The Higher Direction of Combined Operations in the United Kingdom from Dunkirk to Pearl Harbor" by H.J.T. Steers [379]. That covered the time of the Keyes regime. Keyes would remain until October 1941. The biography of Keyes was by Cecil Aspinall-Oglander [14], an Army general who prepared this authorized but uncritical assessment.

In the Lees Knowles Lectures of 1943, Amphibious Warfare and Combined Operations, Keyes [206] reviewed important amphibious operations of the past. In these lectures he referred to the "ill-conceived" Dieppe operation. Glen Barclay [24] wrote an article on Keyes at COHQ. During the summer of 1940 some raids were conducted, including one on the Channel Islands, but little was accomplished. The projects of Keyes appeared increasingly grandiose. Jeremy Langdon [221], "Too Old or Too Bold?: The Removal of Sir Roger Keyes as Churchill's First Director of Combined Operations," reviewed the end for Keyes and some of the controversy. Keyes was already a member of Parliament and remained a backbencher until 1943 when he was created Baron and went to the House of Lords. Joseph Strange [383] has a Maryland dissertation about the debate between the British and Americans over a cross-Channel invasion during 1942. That was one topic discussed when General George Marshall visited London in the spring of 1942. The final decision was to delay the major cross-Channel operation until 1943, delayed again until 1944.

An expansive literature has been forthcoming on Combined Operations, the development of British amphibious warfare operations, and, especially, the origins and development of special or elite forces such as SAS, SBS, Commandos, U.S. Army Rangers, and preparation for what would eventuate as the Normandy invasion of June 1944. To one degree or another, COHQ figured or did not figure, depending on the source and bias of the author, in all of these factors.

Amphibious Warfare: Development in Britain and America from 1920-1940 by Kenneth Clifford [69], an American Marine officer, described the background in the U.S. and Great Britain. There was little cooperation between these future allies, but, together, they advanced faster and further than their enemies. Merrill Bartlett [30] collected 50 articles on the history of amphibious warfare. L.E.H. Maund [265] wrote an early history of combined operations. Sir Bernard Fergusson [124], one of the most important participants, wrote an extensive history, including development of combined operations doctrine in the late 1930s, accounts of early failures such as Norway and Dakar, and the early development of special landing craft and artificial harbors. Two other prominent participants should be mentioned. Canadian Admiral J. Hughes-Hallett [187], advisor to Mountbatten and naval commander of the Dieppe raid, wrote "The Mounting of Raids." Field Marshal Lord Montgomery led in the early planning of the Dieppe raid. The standard biography, three volumes, Monty, was by Nigel Hamilton [153]. Mountbatten was heavily criticized. A later raid, on Bruneval, on the French coast in which an airborne unit seized vital elements of German radar technology, was described by George Millar [271]. Mountbatten wrote the foreword.

Commandos and other elite forces were especially popular topics for writers. The place to begin is Roger Beaumont [33, 34], Special Operations and Elite Units, a research guide. Included was information about Commandos,

Rangers, airborne and submarine special forces, CHINDITS and LRPGs, and later counter-insurgency and counterterror forces. Beaumont also wrote a general survey, Military Elites. Combined Operations [72], The Official Story of the Commandos, with a foreword by Mountbatten, described some of the early operations. Two other accounts of early raids, both with forewords by Mountbatten, were by C.E.L. Phillips [327, 328], The Greatest Raid of All and Cockleshell Heroes. Other general surveys of Commandos and Rangers were by James Ladd [216], with a foreword by Mountbatten, Bill Strutton [386] also with a foreword by Mountbatten, David Hogan [173] with an outstanding bibliographical essay, Richard Garrett [141], who credited Winston Churchill as the originator, Charles Messenger [269], David Thomas [399], John Lorelli [241], John Durnford-Slater [109], a memoir, and Peter Young [441], another legendary Commando leader. The Royal Marines participated in many combined operations, for example, Dieppe. Its history was by James Ladd [217] and Sir Robert Bruce Lockhart [239].

By far the most interest in specific operations executed by COHQ was the Dieppe raid of 19 August 1942. Several months before, 27-28 March 1942, OPERATION CHARIOT, the successful raid against the drydock at St. Nazaire on the French Channel coast was conducted. Its story was told by David Mason [261] in the Ballantine Illustrated History series, H.E. Horan [175], and a French account by A.A.M. Lepotier [228]. The port and drydock, the only one on the coast which could receive one of the German super-battleships, was put out of action for the rest of the war. The periodical After the Battle [335] did a piece on St. Nazaire as it appears now.

THE DIEPPE RAID

The most has been written about the Dieppe raid and much of it reflected outrage and accusations from Canadians, either veterans, historians, or journalists. Mountbatten was blamed. A professor at the University of Ottawa, Brian Loring Villa [413], has proven to his own satisfaction that Mountbatten acted illegally and without authority. Others, including the Mountbatten biographer, Philip Ziegler [448], were not convinced.

Many factors must be considered concerning Dieppe, the French port occupied by the Germans on the Channel coast. Previous raids and actions executed by COHQ had failed. Time was pressing. Operations were less predictable in the fall and winter. Planning by the various services was very complicated, and in the case of Dieppe, the navy withdrew from any planned bombardment before or during the raid by large warships. The air force ruled out bombing by heavy bombers, before or during the raid. The Russians were pressuring heavily for major action in the West to offer relief in the East. Americans were pressuring for offensive action. General George Marshall had made an inspection visit and needed more convincing. The British feared the Americans would abandon the Germany-first strategy if nothing was done. Beaverbrook demanded a "Second Front Now." The Canadians had previously refused to be utilized except as a full unit and had, thus, been inactive for two years. Control over Canadian forces and operations was complex and unclear. The Germans must be attacked and be forced to increase and improve their defenses. The French must be shown that the Allies would liberate them soon. Winston Churchill demanded action or else. Look at what had happened to Roger Keyes. Mountbatten must prove himself. And there must be major preparatory operations for the inevitable full-scale invasion of Fortress Europe.

Literature abounds: Ronald Atkin [16], Herve Cras [87], Ralph Allen [11], Norman Franks [133], Eric Maguire [252], William Whitehead [423], Denis Whitaker [422], Christopher Buckley [49], C.P. Stacey [376], in addition to the Canadian official history, and Earl Mountbatten [290] in a personal account of 1974. There are first-hand accounts: A.B. Austin [17], James Leasor [224], Wallace Reyburn [344], and Quentin Reynolds [345]. Reyburn claimed his was the only eye-witness account.

There were "then and now" studies: Sir James Wilson [426], Peter Henshaw [165], M.R.D. Foot [131], W.G. Ramsey [336], John Campbell [55], Hugh Henry [163], and an article with many photographs in After the Battle [99]. The Henry book also contained many photographs, a photo record from the German perspective.

The latest Canadian account, by Ted Barris [29], presented statistics: 6082 men participated, 4963 of those from the Canadian Second Division, and 3367 casualties, 907 dead and the rest POWs; "the bloodiest nine hours in the Second World War" (p. 19). 5000 Canadians were sacrificed for political, not military, reasons.

Some Canadian accounts were shrill, emotional, anti-British, anti-Mountbatten, and anti-establishment, for example, Barris and Whitaker. The attacks on the naval commander Hughes-Hallet by Wallace Reyburn were so persistent that he threatened legal action.

Three distinguished Canadian professors, Gerald Jordan, Barry Hunt, and Donald Schurman, contributed to a series of essays in honor of Arthur Marder, Jordan [200] being the editor, Naval Warfare in the Twentieth Century. Hunt and Schurman analyzed the planning of the Dieppe raid. This was the period culminating in the British transition from great power to satellite of the U.S. It was also a manifestation of Anglo-American strategic thinking and tensions, Northwest Europe vs. the Mediterranean. British planners were over-optimistic and the forces involved were not prepared for combined operations. Churchill exerted continuous pressure for action. Interservice cooperation and coordination and clearly defined responsibility were lacking. There were too many planners at too many levels. Mountbatten wrote the foreword.

A 40th anniversary commemoration publication, folio size with eight color paintings, was by T.M. Hunter [190] who admitted that valuable experience was attained. The Whitaker piece was a 50th anniversary commemorative publication. Mountbatten wrote the foreword to a book detailing Canadian Victoria Cross and George Cross winners edited by John Swettenham [388].

Ralph Allen called it a tactical failure but a strategic success. Terence Robertson blamed Montgomery. Montgomery blamed the Canadians and Mountbatten. Norman Franks called it the greatest air battle of the war, that is, the British and German fighters dogfighting for 16 hours: 59 British squadrons of fighters flew 3000 sorties; the RAF lost 64 planes and the Germans actually lost only 48 planes, although the British claimed well over a hundred at the time. Sir James Wilson admitted it was tempting but unfair to blame Mountbatten. Reynolds compared Mountbatten to Stonewall Jackson! (p. viii). Mountbatten insisted that the lessons learned meant twelve times less casualties at Normandy. Wallace Reyburn first said lessons were learned for Normandy but later reversed his position. In a book of 1993 Campbell claimed more had been published about Dieppe than about Normandy.

Questions were raised about intelligence leaks and prior knowledge on the part of the Germans. Whitaker claimed he interrogated a German who claimed prior knowledge. The official British naval historian of the war, Stephen Roskill [355], in response to a letter David Irving had written to the Daily Telegraph, 9 September 1963, insisted the documents proved the Germans had not been warned. The exchange of correspondence continued. Beaverbrook raised the level of conflict by printing an article by Irving. Campbell and Foot insisted that there was no German foreknowldege. Prior intelligence for the raiders was another aspect. In Lyman Kirkpatrick [212], Captains without Eyes, Dieppe was used as an example of failures of intelligence.

Brian Villa [413] received an American Historical Association award for his Unauthorized Action. The thesis was that Mountbatten had planned an action against Dieppe, conducted a trial maneuver, and cancelled it. Montgomery had assisted up to that point but pulled out. Mountbatten then proceeded to revive the operation and, without authorization from Churchill and the Chiefs of Staff Committee, executed it. The result was an unmitigated disaster. Villa [412] repeated his claims in an article in 1990. In a review of the book, Philip Ziegler [448] rejected the thesis. In a more recent article, Peter Henshaw [164] contended there was new evidence: Churchill was anxious to pursue offensive operations so he granted Mountbatten new and additional powers. Mountbatten did not need approval from certain higher levels.

SUPREME ALLIED COMMANDER, SOUTHEAST ASIA COMMAND

"Forgotten" was a persistent descriptive term: "forgotten war," "forgotten army," and "forgotten theater." The term applied to the theater, China-Burma-India (C-B-I), one of the three theaters of the Asian/Pacific war. The Germany-first strategy of the Allies and American domination of the Asian/Pacific war meant C-B-I remained at the bottom of the priorities for Allied resources and forces. It was "forgotten." There were grandiose plans for campaigns in Burma, recovery of Singapore, and even massive strategic bombing of the Japanese Home Islands from bases in China. These plans were delayed and, except for the Burma campaign of 1944-1945, ultimately abandoned.

It was this theater over which Mountbatten was appointed Supreme Allied Commander in August 1943. It was predominately a British and Commonwealth (India, Australia, New Zealand, Canada) responsibility. It included China where Chiang Kai-shek seemed more interested in annihilating his Communist opponents than fighting the Japanese. As elsewhere, the Japanese had achieved massive territorial advances during 1942. Most of the Southeast Asia Command (SEAC) area was captured and occupied by Japanese forces. Allied forces were fully committed elsewhere.

Christopher Thorne [403, 404] and Ronald Spector [373] are the best historians who have contributed overviews and backgrounds to the issues of the Asian/Pacific war: Thorne with Allies of a Kind and The Issue of War concentrated on Anglo-American relationships and Spector with Eagle against the Sun presented a comprehensive analysis. Thorne, in Allies of a Kind, stressed that the attack on Pearl Harbor and those Japanese victories during 1942 meant the position of the white man in Asia could never be the same again. He stressed that the Allies had consistently underrated the potential of Japan, that racial tension among the U.S., Great Britain, China, and Japan was an important factor which created crude and condescending images, and that there was a perception that the British cared little about the disposition of China. In The Issue of War, there was more emphasis on societies of Asian states. That related more to the transformation of the postwar Asian/Pacific world. Mountbatten must deal with all of these matters for he remained responsible for C-B-I until late 1946. The subtitle of Eagle against the Sun was The American War against Japan, but it was more than that. Full coverage was allocated to C-B-I, for example, chapter 15, "A Hell of a Beating" (pp. 324-45). He too noted the end of Western political domination of the Far East. The Japanese facilitated the process.

Edward Fischer [126] called it The Chancy War, "chancy" because if you asked for supplies within C-B-I, there was a chance you may get them, but a greater chance you won't (p. 1). As suggested above, The Forgotten War was the title of a series of essays about the British Fourteenth Army of the Far East, "the forgotten army," edited by David Smurthwaite [368]. The Forgotten Army by Peter Ward Fay [123] was actually about the Indian National Army led by Subhas Chandra Bose. It consisted of about 40,000 natives of India, former Japanese POWs from the Malaya-Singapore campaign who were recruited, trained, and integrated into the Japanese army fighting in Burma. It was a total failure as a fighting force but glorified in the imagery of Indian independence. It also has been ignored, Fay contended.

The command structure among the Allies during World War II has been much debated. For the European/Atlantic area, the decision was made in 1942 when General Dwight Eisenhower was made Supreme Allied Commander. The command structure in the Asian/Pacific war was more complicated and problematical. Admiral Chester Nimitz for the Pacific Ocean Area with some subdivisions and General Douglas MacArthur for the Southwest Pacfific Area were appointed early in 1942. No equivalent was created for the rest of the Asian/Pacific theater.

It was at the second Quebec Summit Conference in August 1943 that the pressing matter of command of what became C-B-I was discussed and resolved. At the previous summit conference, third Washington in May 1943, Anglo-American disagreements about the Far East were clear. FDR and Churchill discussed several nominations for commander, for example, Air Marshal Arthur Tedder and Admiral A.B. Cunningham. It was Leo Amery who suggested Mountbatten and there was agreement and a decision for Mountbatten, who was present. Churchill praised Mountbatten, his protege, for being "young, enthusiastic, and triphibious." That quote (p. 143) and the details of the selection were reviewed by J.J. Sbrega [359], "Anglo-American Relations and the Selection of Mountbatten as Supreme Allied Commander, South East Asia." Orde Wingate and the concept of Long Range Penetration Groups or CHINDITS also received sanction. Mountbatten feared the appointment would hurt his naval career but did see it as an opportunity to improve Anglo-American relations. General Joseph Stilwell was made Deputy Commander and the staff commanders were Somerville (Navy), Peirse (Air Force), and Giffard (Army). Most of the vast territory of the command was then under Japanese occupation. A more official perspective can be found in Sir Arthur Bryant [48], A History of the War Years, two volumes, based on the diaries of the Chief of the Imperial General Staff, Lord Alanbrooke.

Charles Canella [57] elaborated in an article. Coalition warfare and control of multinational forces were key factors. But the command apparatus was impossible: five Allied headquarters, that of Stilwell for the U.S., the British in India, the Chinese forces located in India, Chiang in China, and Mountbatten, ultimately in Kandy, Ceylon. Mountbatten directed a team of four commanders-in-chief of three services and two nationalities, all senior to him. No Chinese were on the staff. Personality conflicts abounded: Stilwell vs. Chennault, Mountbatten vs. Somerville, Chiang vs. Stilwell, and Mountbatten vs. Stilwell. Donald Macintyre [250] wrote a biography of Somerville. H.P.

Willmott [424, 425] published a book in 1995 from an Oxford dissertation about a "forgotten" navy, the British navy in the Far East, and the difficulty formulating a strategy due to a bitter debate between Churchill and the naval planners

Mountbatten [295] himself addressed the Royal United Services Institute in London in October 1946 on the command. He made observations about the confusion and overlapping responsibilities. His [293] official report to his superiors, the Combined Chiefs of Staff, an Anglo-American military command, was published. Mountbatten [291] also anticipated postwar tasks in second report to the Combined Chiefs. There were 120,000 Allied POWs to be repatriated and 700,000 Japanese to be processed and sent home. Return of European colonial administrations, for example, the British, French, and Dutch, was particularly problematical. The impressive British historian of these matters, Louis Allen [9], wrote a survey of the Japanese occuption of Southeast Asia, a supplement to the Mountbatten [292] report. Allen described in detail events in Indochina, the British and Chinese forces entering and the return of the French in the south. Allen [8] elaborated on all of this in a book published in the late 1970s. A new map of Asia was the result.

This process of decolonization produced enormous complications and consequences. The U.S. was in the dominant position and the U.S. had demonstrated determination to end all empires since early in the war. In the brilliant Making of the Twentieth Century series, B.N. Pandey [319], South and South-East Asia. Fourteen new countries will emerge from former empires. A.S.B. Olver [310] described British policy over the first five postwar years. In two works, Nicholas Tarling [391, 392], analyzed the factors concerning the end of empire in the region for the British.

A distinguished Australian historian, Peter Dennis [97] produced Troubled Days of Peace: Mountbatten and the South-East Asia Command. He concentrated on the crucial postwar years, 1945-1946. Japan surrendered while some of South Asia and most of Southeast Asia were still occupied. The task was daunting and Mountbatten was responsible. Mountbatten took the formal surrender of the Japanese at Singapore on 12 September 1945, almost a month after the Japanese surrender was first announced. The forces and logistics were grossly inadequate for the task. He was dependent on MacArthur for shipping and MacArthur was not always forthcoming. Nationalist rebels had been encouaged and assisted by the Japanese. Frequently, the surrendering Japanese turned over their arms to the nationalist rebels. Some nationalists declared independence. Most had collaborated with the Japanese. To add further complications, the area of SEAC was increased substantially at the end of the war, increasing the responsibilities of Mountbatten. Stilwell, Albert Wedemeyer, the successor to Stilwell, MacArthur, and Admiral Ernest King were all anglophobes. It was Mountbatten who called them "troubled days of peace" (p. 2).

Recall the KELLY Reunion Association. A similar nostalgic motivation must have been the basis for "Where I Came In. . . ." in China, Burma, India, edited by R.J. Kadel [202], a folio size picture album format incorporating several objectives. The narrative section was extensive: stories, articles, memorials, recollections, and a poem to "The Admiral." There was a photo of Mountbatten opposite the dedication page: "To SAC Lord Lewis [sic] Mountbatten," but "Lord Louis" elsewhere in the text. Other features included tributes and memorials to Wingate, who was buried in Arlington Cemetary, Stilwell, Philip Cochran, the model for "Terry and the Pirates" (the Flying Tigers), Hump flyers, and an article by Frank Owen as a tribute to Mountbatten: "his charm, his energy, his sense of urgency;" a man of purpose, the youngest Captain in the Royal Navy of his time, younger than Nelson, and the youngest Admiral of the Royal Navy of all time (p. 150).

And there was the China-Burma-India Hump Pilots Association which published a nostalgic, two-volume, folio size album covering their reunions of 1980 in Poplar Bluff, MO and 1981 in Milwaukee. The editor was James Brewer [42]. The association began in 1946. Included was a mini-biography of Mountbatten (p. 510).

Several other sources focused on Mountbatten as commander of C-B-I. In his history of logistics in warfare, Julian Thompson [402], the British general who was in command of some operations in the Falklands/Malvinas campaign of 1982, used the case study of the Burma campaign of 1943-1945 "as perhaps the logistic triumph of the Second World War" (p. xii). He praised Mountbatten who ordered the campaign to continue through the monsoon season, making the issue of logistics even more critical, and still succeeding. Thurzal Terry [398], an American bombardier of the 10th Air Force, devoted a chapter to Mountbatten (pp. 65-71), an extremely popular and capable commander, skillful at soothing Anglo-American relations. Hank Nelson [309] wrote of the feelings and anxieties of Australian POWs scattered all over Southeast Asia, some not freed until October of 1945. James Leasor [225] described a special, secret mission in India. German U-boats were operating in the Indian Ocean, guided from a secret transmitter on the coast. In March 1943 the transmitter was blown up and sinkings were immediately reduced.

The "China" in C-B-I elicited some literature. One of the well-known "Old China Hands," John Paton Davies, Jr. [95], wrote about modern American, British, Japanese, and Russian encounters with China and with one another. It was helpful and informative for context and perspective. Davies incorporated a kind of calculus of interrelationships of all of these states. It was most enlightening on the Stilwell-Chiang controversy and on the agenda and decisions at the Cairo Summit Conference of November 1943 involving FDR, Churchill, Chiang, and Mountbatten. The China-Burma-India Theater, a three-volume addition to the highly respected The U.S. Army in World War II official history series, by Charles Romanus [350], presented the best summary of American operations in the theater and especially the full story of the role of Stilwell. Barbara Tuchman [411] won her second Pulitzer Prize, this one for 1972, for her biography of Stilwell. Against the advice of General Marshall, FDR recalled Stilwell in 1944 and replaced him with General Albert Wedemeyer. Keith Eiler [114] edited selected documents from the Wedemeyer papers, located at the Hoover Institution, as are the Stilwell papers.

The "Burma" elicited even more literature. Important land and air campaigns occurred here throughout the war. The Japanese overran it relatively easily, 1942-1943. Then the British with some American and even Chinese assistance, drove the Japanese out, 1944-1945, in the worst defeat suffered by the Japanese in the war. Mountbatten was Supreme Commander but General William Slim, commander of the 14th Army was credited with the final victory. In the process, Orde Wingate and the innovative LRPG tactics created much comment and strong criticism, especially from established and traditional commanders. The transfer of power after the war was complicated and an independent Burma did not remain in the Commonwealth, a serious failure.

Slim's [365] own account, Defeat into Victory, was considered to be a classic of military literature. There were several biographies: by Ronald Lewin [233], by Sir Geoffrey Evans [117] in the Military Commander series, and by Michael Calvert [54] in the Ballantine Illustrated History series. Mountbatten publically praised Slim as the best general of the war.

Frank Owen [312] wrote the summary report of the Burma campaign on the part of the Southeast Asian Command. Two more extensive and scholarly surveys of the Burma campaign were by Louis Allen [7], with the subtitle The Longest War, and Raymond Callahan [53]. The decisive battles of the campaign were at Arakan, Imphal, and Kohima, forcing the attacking Japanese to cease their "March on Delhi," to invade India. These key events were covered by A.J. Barker [25] who interviewed Japanese commanders, Lucas Phillips [329], Geoffrey Matthews [264], and David Rooney [352].

Much controversy and an expansive literature arose over Orde Wingate, the CHINDITS, and their American counterpart, Merrill's Marauders, and the tactic of Long Range Penetration Groups which operated in Burma in 1943-1944. They exploited the advantages of air power and superior communications and were able to disrupt enemy held territory far from their own lines. Problems developed such as numerous and severe health and fatigue cases. Russel Prather [333], Shelford Bidwell [37], The Chindit War, and Charles Hunter [189], GALAHAD, were histories of the operations. Hunter was successor to Frank Merrill of Merrill's Marauders, the American unit. A new biography of Wingate by Trevor Royle [358] reviewed the operations, assessed the results, analyzed the "myths," and reviewed the debate over the controversy. Most sensational was the direct criticism of Wingate and LRPGs in the official British history of the war, by Woodburn Kirby [210]. Mountbatten praised the CHINDITS as outstanding examples of interservice cooperation, but he called Wingate a pain in the neck.

Wingate was killed in an air crash in 1944 at age 41. David Rooney [353] and Sir Bernard Fergusson [125] surveyed the literature of the debate.

"Transfer of power" was a term used to describe the gaining of independence of colonies. The next chapter will be devoted to the process in the case of India and Mountbatten viewed that case, perhaps rightly, as a triumph. In the case of Burma he was not so confident and proud. He was not pleased with the actions of British colonial officials, especially the pre-war Governor, Sir Reginald Dorman-Smith and the Chief Civil Affairs Officer, General Pearce, both of whom returned to administer Burma upon liberation from Japanese occupation. They had been out of touch with events and affairs. So were their superiors in London. For example, they saw prominent nationalist leaders such as Aung San, who had collaborated with the Japanese, as criminals. Over twenty were executed. Ultimately, the transfer of power took place and Burma refused to join the British Commonwealth. Mountbatten blamed himself for this failure. Mountbatten wanted to cooperate more with Burmese nationalists. These matters were reviewed by Louis Allen [10] and Nicholas Tarling [392] who concluded that there was little chance of success.

The official study of events in Burma between January 1944 to January 1948 was exhaustive, two volumes edited by Hugh Tinker [405]. The British government sponsored a number of these "transfer of power" studies and this one was much praised for thoroughness and comprehensiveness, for example, by Louis Allen [10]. The background of Anglo-Burmese relations, from 1752-1948, was reviewed by U Htin Aung [184], although consistently partisan toward Burma. Hugh Tinker [408] took up the story there, describing the first years of independence. Burmese Nationalist Movements by U. Maung Maung [266] reviewed periods of British colonialism, the rise of Burmese nationalism, especially the Anti-Fascist People's Freedom League (AFPFL) led by Aung San, the Japanese occupation, liberation, and the transfer of power. Aung San was assassinated in July 1947 and was succeeded by U Nu. The winner of the Nobel Peace Prize, Aung San Suu Kyi [214], wrote a biography of her father in the Leaders of Asia series.

The "India" of China-Burma-India will be reviewed in the next chapter. Mountbatten moved from SAC SEAC to Viceroy of India, the last Viceroy before the transfer of power in August 1947.

Meantime, it was a different story for Indochina, subsequently broken up into Vietnam, Cambodia, and Laos. This had been a French colony since the 1850s. FDR vowed to end colonization, one of his war aims for World War II. He is alleged to have ranked the various colonial powers and concluded that the French were the worst, and that they should not be permitted to regain their colonies after the war. Collaboration with the Germans during the war did not help the reputation of France. Nevertheless, other factors obviously prevailed because FDR himself began to waver. After his death in April 1945, Harry Truman then agreed to assist the French to return to Indochina, which they did.

In the spring of 1945 the Japanese seized control of Indochina from Vichy French collaborating colonial administrators. They encourage various nationalist groups and assisted them. The war ended in August/September. The Potsdam Agreement provided that the British would be responsible for liberating South Vietnam with its capital at Saigon. A temporary military demarcation line at 16 degrees North Latitude was to divide Vietnam. In the North, originally, Chinese forces were to move in. That part was subsequently changed. Ronald Spector [372] produced a piece about conflicts and confusion of Allied intelligence related to these times. American aid had been going to Ho and other anti-Japanese nationalists. Anglo-American disagreement and confusion about American objectives exacerbated an already complex situation.

OPERATION MASTERDOM provided for a British occupation force to facilitate repatriation of the Japanese and restore order. British D. Gracey and a force of mostly Indian troops landed. There were problems. Gracey was said to have exceeded orders and facilitated the return of the French in the South. Peter Dunn [106, 107] prepared a Nevada dissertation on OPERATION MASTERDOM and followed it with a book, The First Vietnam War, which recounted the return of the French, increasing tensions with nationalist movements, and ultimately open warfare, especially with the Viet Minh led by Ho Chi Minh. They took over in the North, fought the French, and defeated them in 1954 when the French withdrew. That was the First Vietnam War. The U.S. began paying for the French action and took over all responsibility after 1954. Review of the vast literature on that would not be germane here.

"Britain and the Transfer of Power in Indonesia, 1945-1945" was a London dissertation by C.W. Squire [375]. Again this was an area under the responsibility of Mountbatten and the process involved the Japanese in full occupation at the end, their prior encouragement and support to nationalist groups, and British forces facilitating the return of Dutch colonial administrators and armed forces. As in Indochina it was an imbroglio. An interesting story was told by Laurens van der Post [332], The Admiral's Baby, about a British agent who remained in Indonesia after the war to facilitate British liberation operations and the return of the Dutch. He had contacts with nationalists leaders. Post was first sent to Mountbatten in Ceylon to explain the complex situation. Mountbatten sent him on to London and London sent him to persuade the Dutch to use restraint as they returned. The "Admiral's Baby" referred to a particularly ruthless and insensitive Dutch admiral, Patterson. A long war of independence ensued.

The situation in Malaya was different. Simon Smith [367] of the University of London reviewed British-Malay relations, 1930-1957. The decolonization process was more deliberate, slower, and ended in Commonwealth status. The British SOE had initiated secret infiltration operations during the Japanese occupation, Force 136, which was based in Ceylon. 371 British personnel had infiltrated and armed and trained over 3000 guerrillas.

Mountbatten wrote the foreword for that and for an individual case study of one of the British operatives, John Cross [88].

7

Works about Mountbatten, Viceroy and Governor-General of India

The "India" of China-Burma-India was different. Although the Japanese conducted a major offensive beginning in 1944, the Road to Delhi campaign, with the objective of overrunning India, they failed, were forced back, and surrendered in September 1945. It was the worst defeat ever experienced by the Japanese army. So, unlike Burma and China, India was never occupied by Japanese forces. But India was very much in the war and India was the most important colony of Great Britain. The armed forces of Britain in India, many of whom were Indian natives, increased from 200,000 to over two million. Indian territory was utilized for bases for supplying Lend-Lease aid to China on a massive scale, for bases of Allied, mostly American, bombers, including, for a moment, the first B-29 Superfortress bombers used in the war. They flew a few sorties, for example, bombing Bangkok, but were soon moved to Saipan in the Central Pacific Theater, from where strategic and fire bombing of Japan originated.

The colonial/decolonization factor must also be considered. The Americans were demanding decolonization. FDR sent at least two special missions to India to facilitate the process toward independence. But Churchill was equally determined to perpetuate British rule in India, what was called the Raj. The Congress Party of Indian nationalists opposed the war and launched a "Quit India" campaign. Most of the leaders were arrested and spent the rest of the war in jail.

The pertinent volumes in the distinguished Making of the Twentieth Century series were Britain and Decolonisation by John Darwin [92], a chronological survey which presented the international context, analysis of the official mind, and details on colonial nationalist movements, and B.N. Panay [318], The Break-up of British India, who concluded that separation created problems but solved none. Darwin concluded that overall, Great Britain decolonized with grace, not as a "weary titan." The British Raj in India by

Samuel Burke [50] was a scholarly review of the history. Judith Brown [47] of Oxford University, Modern India, in the Short Oxford History of the Modern World series introduced the issues and placed events in India in context. The noted historian, Michael Edwardes [112], discussed crucial events prior to the transfer.

The official and most extensive study, Transfer of Power, 12 volumes, was edited by Nicholas Mansergh [255], bringing together all of the pertinent documents. Prime Minister Harold Wilson accelerated the release time, originally to be 1999. The last three volumes, X-XII, 3400 pages, were devoted to the Mountbatten Viceroyalty. Others writing on this matter were V.P. Menon [267, 268], a participant with two related works, C.H. Philips [326], H.M. Seervai [360], S.S. Hamid [152], with a foreword by Philip Ziegler, H.V. Hudson [185], Anita Inder Singh [191], and Sir Penderel Moon [276]. A Muslim perspective was presented by Maulana Abul Kalam Azad [18], an official who favored a united India. He failed to convince his co-religionists. He dedicated this memoir to Nehru.

Philips noted that Mountbatten was reluctant to go to India, fearing disruption of his naval career, and was able to negotiate and gain extraordinary powers from the Labor government before he went to India. Philips also concluded that division was inevitable and the role of Mountbatten has been exaggerated.

In July 1945, in what was called a "Khaki" election, the Conservative government of Churchill was defeated and replaced by a Labor government headed by Clement Attlee. It was left to the Attlee government to decolonize India, which they proceeded to do. This was where Mountbatten, and Lady Mountbatten with him now, entered the picture. Other personalities of most significance were Indian nationalists, Gandhi, Nehru, and Jinnah, two previous Viceroys, Earl Wavell and Lord Linlilthgow, and the military commander, General Auchinlech.

Sir Stafford Cripps, representing the British Cabinet, came to India to offer Dominion status, January-April 1942. One FDR mission intervened at this point. Sir Reginald Coupland [83, 84] produced two surveys of the Cripps Mission. "The U.S. and the Indian Crisis, 1941-1943: The Limits of Anti-Colonialism," by P.D. Garlock [139], was a Yale dissertation with the conclusion that FDR ultimately refused to jeopardize the Anglo-American alliance to fulfill anti-colonial objectives. Churchill, Cripps, and India by R.J. Moore [277], focused on the powerful influence of the opposition by Churchill, even when he was out of office, and his ability to sabotage policies.

Mountbatten met with Gandhi six times, but Gandhi continued to support a united India. Mountbatten was credited with convincing Sadar Patel, a prominent Congress Party official, to favor partition, and then, slowly, Nehru. Azad concluded that Lady Mountbatten contributed in the process of changing the views of Nehru (p. 215). Azad lamented the "rivers of blood" which flowed at the time of partition. His work was also dedicated to Nehru. Inder Singh focused on the Muslim League, the equivalent to the Congress Party, representing the Muslims. She insisted that Jinnah was not the mouthpiece of the League. Moon stressed what others also observed: the British had followed a practice for a century by "divide and rule," so it was natural to "divide and quit."

The literature on the role of Mountbatten in the process was expansive and demonstrated the degree of the controversy which has arisen. Indeed, there were a series of critiques, apologetics, and further critiques, each a response to the other. Mountbatten [287, 288, 315] himself left three recollections: Mountbatten and Independent India, Mountbatten and Pakistan, and an essay in Pakistan: Past and Present. The last entry was a commemoration of the centenary of the birth of Jinnah. Mountbatten recalled his personal interviews and negotiations with Jinnah. There was also a TV documentary, "The Last Viceroy" [222], which fairly depicted events. The official biography by Philip Ziegler [445] has been cited above in the chapter on biographies. Part III, chapters 28-37 (pp. 349-482), was devoted to Mountbatten and India. The title of the first chapter was "The Most Important Journey." Details of the process followed. The Campbell-Johnson [56] account complemented that of Ziegler and has also been cited earlier; mostly apologetics. Total defeatism prevailed among the leadership. The Viceroy, Wavell, had utterly failed. Lord Ismay noted that only Mountbatten, and no one else, could have done it. Attlee called in Mountbatten who negotiated more personal power to accomplish the task. This was the summary presented by Sir James Wilson [427].

Was Mountbatten responsible for the massacres which followed the transfer and separation? A running commentary can be reviewed. Leonard Mosley [281] and R.J. Moore [279], in an article in 1981, answered yes. Partition and thus the communal violence could have been avoided if Mountbatten had taken more time. Gandhi, who opposed partition, observed to Mountbatten: "you and your magic tricks" (Moore p. 38). Mosley recalled that 1947 "was a bumper year for vultures" (p. 243). Y. Krishnan [213] agreed in an article in 1983. The transfer of power was too hurried and premature. Mountbatten was even accused of accelerating the date so he could hurry home in time for a royal wedding later in 1947 (p. 22). What was important to Mountbatten was to secure Indian membership in the Commonwealth. I.A. Talbot [390] responded to Krishnan in an article in 1984. British control was being undermined rapidly. Mountbatten arrived in India in the spring of 1947 and immediately concluded the British could not hold on into 1948, a decisive factor not considered by Krishnan. Politicians in the Punjab manipulated communal tensions and should be blamed for the violence. In another article, unrelated to those just cited, Ian Copland [80] denied Mountbatten had achieved "a personal triumph." His contribution was not so impressive. He abandoned the powerful Indian princes and settled the question with the Congress Party (pp. 394-404). Sir Conrad Corfield [81] also was an advocate for the Indian princes.

Manmath Nath Das [93], touting "the inside story of the Mountbatten days," recalled the incomprehensible chaos of events and speculated on what Winston Churchill and Jinnah may have done behind the scenes. The Pakistani perspective was presented by Latif Ahmed Sherwani [361]. Larry Collins [70, 71] and Dominique Lapierre have collaborated on a wide variety of popular histories from Hitler's order to burn Paris to Spanish bullfighting. In books published in the mid-1970s and mid-1980s, they assessed the transfer of power and the role of Mountbatten. They claimed they had conducted 500 interviews including thirty hours on tape with Mountbatten, 600 transcribed pages, and the two daughters. The root of the problem of India was the antagonism between 300,000,000 Hindus and 100,000,000 Moslems, exacerbated by the British policy of divide and rule. In addition to their simplistic analysis, they exaggerated the role of Mountbatten.

The Attlee government appointed Mountbatten Viceroy, he went to India, ten weeks later he announced that transfer would occur in ten weeks, not June of 1948 as previously planned. Transfer and partition were the result. Mountbatten was the last Viceroy. But this was not solely the work of Mountbatten. Some critics believe his role has been exaggerated. Other personalities were just as or more important.

Hugh Tinker [406, 407] had produced scholarly assessments of the events of the transfer and a series of mini-biographies of many of the chief personalities. The former was sponsored by the Royal Institute of International Affairs. Tinker praised the achievement of Mountbatten, who did a difficult job well. The latter consisted of eight published lectures, each a biographical essay of nationalist leaders responsible for the transfer of power, including Nehru and Jinnah.

In that regard, the name of Jawaharlal Nehru (1889-1964) was frequently mentioned. He was the recognized leader of the Congress Party, representing the majority of Indian citizens. He must be convinced to support separation, and he was. There were at least four good biographies, one published in 1997: Stanley Wolpert [435], extensively researched and containing personal details, for example, on affairs with Lady Mountbatten and Claire Booth Luce, and even a flirtation with Jackie Kennedy. The biography by Sarvepalli Gopal [146] was three volumes with an abridged edition published in 1993. It was an authorized biography backed by a research team and granted full access to papers. The emphasis was on foreign policy, for example, growing tensions with China. Michael Edwardes [113] and Michael Brecher [41], both with subtitles A Political Biography, have published biographies of Nehru. The Nehru Memorial Trust was set up by Mountbatten soon after the death of Nehru in 1964. Annual Nehru Memorial Lectures have been presented in Britain, fifteen of them already given at the time a description was published by John Grigg [148] in 1992. It was Nehru who insisted that Mountbatten remain in India as Governor-General. Mountbatten reluctantly agreed and remained into 1948.

Clearly, next in importance was Muhammad Ali Jinnah (1876-1948), the leader of the Muslim League and the first President of Pakistan. Biographies and studies were by Stanley Wolpert [434], demonstrating extensive research, Ayesha Jalal [194], who claimed Jinnah was originally against partition, Chaudri Muhammad Ali [6], and Akbar Ahmed [2], noting Jinnah was enigmatic and inscrutible. Akbar Ahmed resented the negative depictions of Jinnah, for example, in the movie, "Gandhi" [137], directed by Richard Attenborough. Akbar Ahmed [3], a Cambridge professor, elaborated in an article of 1996, "The Hero in History: Myth, Media, and Realities," citing the case study of Jinnah. Mountbatten was a brilliant manipulator of the media, as was Nehru. Together, they had managed to portray Jinnah as a villain. They had actually used terms to describe Jinnah such as psychopath, lunatic, snob, and megalomaniac. Mountbatten called him "a bastard." Mountbatten was upset because his famous charm was rebuffed by Jinnah. About the love affair between Lady Mountbatten and Nehru: "Nehru appeared to command the Viceroy's office through his bedroom" (p. 10). Ziegler had little to say about it and the Gopal [146] biography ignored it.

The two previous Viceroys have been subjects of studies. Baron John Glendevon [144] and Gowher Rizvi [347] wrote on Lord Linlithgow, Viceroy, 1936-1943, who had brought India into World War II, and Ronald Lewin wrote on Earl Archibald Wavell [231], Viceroy, 1943-1947. Wavell's [417] own journal as Viceroy was also published. The Attlee government suddenly dumped Wavell and turned to Mountbatten.

Attlee himself and his government, 1945-1951, were the subjects of some works. Jerry Brookshire [45] published a biography in 1995. There was a chapter on the empire and Commonwealth. An earlier biography was by Kenneth Harris [157], with a section on the end of empire. Attlee underestimated the influence of Jinnah and the Muslims. Nick Tiratsoo [409] edited The Attlee Years, eleven essays by experts, two of which were about India. The Attlee cabinet was divided on the issue. The matter of the British government reducing the length of national service from 18 to 12 months, deemed decisive by Mountbatten, was stressed. The appointment of Mountbatten was a coup of the Labor government. R.J. Moore [278] reviewed the Indian policies of the Labor government, 1946-1947. It recognized the unbridgeable chasm between the Congress Party and the Muslim League. The unfortunate Indian princes were hoodwinked. N.J. Owen [313] wrote an Oxford dissertation on the Labor Party and the Indian problem. Philip Warner [415] wrote a biography of General Auchinleck, the commander-in-chief of British forces during the mid-1940s.

Always influential in the background, but with no official position as with all the ones reviewed above, was Mahatma Gandhi. His relations with Mountbatten and Wavell were surveyed by Francis Watson [416]. The Gandhi-Mountbatten relationship was described as "uninhibited friendliness" (p. 96). The popular and successful movie "Gandhi" [137] has been mentioned. It won eight Academy Awards. Directed by Richard Attenborough and dedicated to Nehru and Mountbatten, it was clearly critical of Jinnah, depicting him as devious.

8

Works about Mountbatten, First Sea Lord and Chief of Defense Staff

When Mountbatten was appointed to Combined Operations, to SAC SEAC, to Viceroy, and the Governor-General of India, he was always reluctant and consistently concerned that his primary objective, a naval career leading to the top professional position in the navy, First Sea Lord, would be jeopardized. His father achieved that office but then lost it in a humiliating manner.

So, at the first possible opportunity after his commitment to services as SAC SEAC and in India were completed, he returned to Great Britain, resumed his permanent rank of Rear Admiral, and returned to his professional naval career, first as a Crusier Squadron Commander in the Mediterranean fleet. He later served as Fourth Sea Lord, and finally, April 1955-April 1959, First Sea Lord. It was a crucial time for the postwar Royal Navy. The Royal Air Force was being seen increasingly as the first line of defense, its super-bombers and missiles being given priority as vehicles for nuclear weaponry. Naval forces were too vulnerable in the nuclear age. Mountbatten actually opposed Great Britain acquiring an independent nuclear capability, to no avail.

The essence of these matters was articulated in the White Paper of 1957 during the ministerial regime of Duncan Sandys. It was dubbed "the New Look." M.S. Navias [308] has a London dissertation and Wyn Rees [343] an article summarizing the provisions and effects of the new policy. Mandatory service ended, conventional weapons were downgraded, and nuclear weapons were upgraded. The navy lost much funding support.

Yet the Defence White Paper of 1958, while Mountbatten was still First Sea Lord, reversed the trend and the navy gained status and new capabilities associated with nuclear weapons. Mountbatten was credited with the turnaround. Mountbatten was also establishing closer relations with his counterparts in the U.S. Navy, Admirals Arleigh Burke and Hyman Rickover. This would lead to significant access by the British, first to the nuclear propulsion system and later to the Polaris ballistic missile system, developed by the Americans. The "Special Relationship" was alive and well. All of these matters were reviewed in The

First Sea Lords: From Fisher to Mountbatten, edited by Malcolm Murfett [304], the Mountbatten essay being written by Geoffrey Till (pp. 265-82).   David Brown [46] wrote an article on Mountbatten as First Sea Lord. Anglo-American relations and the Special Relationship were reviewed by John Charmley [68], Churchill's Grand Alliance, S.J. Ball [22], and Stephen Hastings [160].

Admiral Sir Ian McGeoch [247], a naval leader of the 1990s, was distressed about cut-backs and closing of bases. He recalled the 1950s when there were similar crises and Mountbatten had initiated the "Way Ahead Committee" to institute reforms, and they were significant, comparable to the great Fisher reforms of the early twentieth century. McGeoch mockingly recommended "The Way Astern Committee."

The theoretical, strategic, and military aspects of these postwar times were debated extensively. British Military Thought after World War II, by Julian Lider [234], and a Princeton dissertation and related book on British defense policy into the 1960s by William Snyder [369, 370] reviewed general trends while William Crowe [89], A.C. Hampshire [154], and John Woods [436] all focused strictly on the Royal Navy during the same time, from about 1945 into the early 1960s.   Admiral William Crowe was later U.S. ambassador to Great Britain. Phillip Darby [90, 91] has an Oxford dissertation and book on British defense policy east of Suez, an important factor related to British imperial and international obligations. Mountbatten was the chief naval voice during much of this time.

Mountbatten also used his royal and international connections in furthering Anglo-American cooperation in the development of nuclear capabilities, both propulsion, eventually used most effectively in nuclear powered submarines, and later nuclear weapons, in the navy case, the Polaris missile system. The matter of developments of nuclear capabilities meant a decisive advancement in strategic roles for the navy, and at the expense of the air force. These matters were discussed by John Simpson [363], Nicholas Wheeler [419], M.S. Navias [307], Colin McInnes [249], I.J. Galatin [136], Andrew Pierre [330], Peter Nailor [306], and Theodore Rockwell [349].   Rockwell wrote of the spectacular achievements of Admiral Rickover and the development of nuclear propulsion plants for warships. Nailor described the Nassau Agreement of 1962 between President John Kennedy and Prime Minister Harold Macmillan, providing Polaris missiles for British nuclear submarines.

Meantime, the most serious crisis of the postwar era for the British occurred and the Special Relationship was seriously strained. This was the Suez Crisis of 1956, seen as the last dying gasp of British--and French--imperialism. President Nassar of Egypt nationalized the Suez Canal in the summer of 1956. There were objections from all of the Western powers but no immediate action was taken. The Prime Minister, Anthony Eden, began secret plans, coordinated with the French and, though he denied it to Parliament and the public at the time, Israel. In the fall Israel declared war and commenced operations against

Egypt and a joint British-French expeditionary force attacked Egypt. The military operations generally achieved initial goals. It was the international, especially the American, reaction against what was dubbed naked colonialism which soon caused the operations to be halted and withdrawal executed. Mountbatten was First Sea Lord and he opposed the operation. The navy did perform the necessary functions and performed well under the circumstances.

The literature on Suez was extensive. General surveys included those by Hugh Thomas [401], Keith Kyle [215], Andre Beaufre [32], Roy Fullick [135], A.J. Barker [26], Anthony Moncrieff [275], Anthony Adamthwaite [1], and Howard Dooley [102]. An Exeter dissertation by D.A. Al-Solami [12] covered the political and military preparations. W.S. Lucas [242, 243, 244] produced three studies, one a London dissertation on the American reaction and imperial implications. The published diaries of Evelyn Shuckburgh [362], an important official of the Foreign Office, were an indictment of the highest leadership in the fiasco: "conceived in deceit and arrested in pusillanimity" (p. 366). Shuckburgh also observed deterioration in the Prime Minister. Eden's [111] own memoirs were published and an authorized biography was written by Robert Rhodes James [346]. Details of a secret meeting of British, French, and Israelis at Severes were published. Eden had openly lied to Parliament and now it was all exposed.

The capstone of the professional achievements of Mountbatten, some claimed his most significant accomplishment, was initiation of unification of the armed services of Great Britain, first begun in the 1950s. He was made Chief of the Defence Staff in July 1959 and served two and a half terms until 1964 when he retired permanently from the service. Franklyn Johnson [195, 196], an American professor, was the historian first of British imperial defense and then of the unification of the services into the Ministry of Defence. Johnson [197, 198] then wrote two essays on the role of Mountbatten in the latter, the unification of the services. This was a major restructuring and reorganization of the armed forces. Duplication was reduced and efficiency improved. Johnson noted that the true test was the Falklands/Malvinas campaign of 1982, two decades later.

John Gooch [145] presented a chronological survey of the higher organization of British defense in the twentieth century. Lessons obviously needed to be learned from the Boer War, 1900-1903. John Sweetman [387] surveyed civil-military relations during the same period; Sir Ewen Broadbent [43] similarly, but for the 1950s through the 1980s. His focus was on the army. Some restructuring had begun at the time of the Korean War, as describe by J.G. Albert [4]. Michael Howard [182], The Central Organisation of Defence, concentrated on Mountbatten as CDS and the reforms initiated by him. In a set of biographical essays similar to the compilation by Malcolm Murfett [304] on First Sea Lords, Sir William Jackson [193] collected essays on the Chiefs of Staff, the top military leaders. Chapter 10 (pp. 309-50) was on the Mountbatten era culminating in the Ministry of Defence. That era ended with the arrival of a Labor government in 1964 and the defense regime of Denis Healey, as presented by Bruce Reed [342]. Mountbatten remained as CDS for several months but he chose not to oppose the Healey innovations and cut-backs, for example, a super-carrier. Dry Ginger by Richard Baker [20] was the biography of Admiral Sir Michael Le Fanu, First Sea Lord and CDS after Mountbatten. The title referred to the occasion of abolition of the rum ration in the Royal Navy which occurred on his "watch."

9

Retirement and Death of Earl Mountbatten

Mountbatten retired as CDS and from the active navy in 1965. Almost immediately he was asked by the Home Office to conduct an investigation of the security of British prisons. There had been several escapes of a sensational nature. Mountbatten conducted the investigation and published its report [294], Report of the Inquiry into Prison Escapes and Security.

Mountbatten personally wrote at least 70 forewords, prefaces, and introductions to a wide variety of books. He was also an author. Some examples of his publications are as follows. His earliest effort was published under a pseudonym, MARCO [257, 258], An Introduction to Polo, first published in 1930 with many subsequent editions, and The Spectator at Polo. He published articles [66, 67] in Chakkar, a magazine about polo. These activities, driving fast cars, and the international travel projected the public image as playboy. The fast cars factor was reviewed in Richard Garrett [140] Motoring and the Mighty. For the French magazine Paris Match, 21 August 1965, Mountbatten [285] wrote a nine-page article in French of his experiences during World War II. Mountbatten [286] had an extensive picture album published: Mountbatten: Eighty Years in Pictures, over 200 pages, in 1979.

Solly Zuckerman [449] and others described the Cecil King affair of 1968 in which Mountbatten was sought out to consider heading a coalition government to replace the Wilson government. Stephen Dorril [103], Smear, wrote in some detail about this imbroglio. Zuckerman was able to get permission from Mountbatten to attend a secret meeting where plans and possiblities were to be discussed. The ambitions of King were extreme and Mountbatten was persuaded to dismiss all thoughts of becoming involved. Zuckerman called it "rank treachery" (p. 179). Nothing came of it.

Mountbatten was invited to Canada to make an important address, a curious event in light of much emotional feeling against Mountbatten by Canadians. The Empire Club of Canada [115] published the speech, "The Unsinkable Commonwealth" at the Centennial Dinner, 11 July 1967.

Electronics the Lifeline [284], sponsored by the National Electronics Council, was a lecture Mountbatten delivered in June 1978 at the Royal Institution. Apocalypse Now?: Earl Mountbatten, Lord Noel Baker, Lord Zuckerman [282] was a pamphlet which included a speech presented by Mountbatten, "The Final Abyss?", at a special assembly on disarmament. The occasion was the award of the Louise Weiss Foundation Prize to the Stockholm International Peace Research Institute, Strasbourg, France, 11 May 1979.

Mountbatten gave the major address at the annual Jutland dinner in 1978. It was published [283] in Mariner's Mirror. He recalled his arrival aboard HMS LION, Admiral Beatty's flagship, seven weeks after the battle. It was his first sea assignment. He observed that the Germans had built battle cruisers which had lighter guns, less speed, but with better protection. Nine gun turrets of German ships had been pierced but none blew up. British losses during the battle were due to design defects, no planning, and no Staff College, Mountbatten concluded.

The assassination of Mountbatten was a sensational shock. Reaction was rapid and expansive. Obituaries appeared in many newspapers and journals, for example, in Mariner's Mirror [303], November 1979, by E.F. Gueritz, President. He was patron of the sponsor, the Society of Naval Research, and there were plans for a special tribute on the occasion of his 80th birthday and the 30th year of his Patronage. Prince Philip succeeded Mountbatten in 1980. Mountbatten's father was President of SNR, 1911-1921, and had launched the Save the VICTORY Fund.

Published in 1981 was a book in French by Roger Faligot [122], Nous avons tue Mountbatten: L'IRA parle, including a series of interviews with an IRA commander about his role in the assassination. Other events which coincided with the assassination were 81 hunger strikes of jailed IRA members and other bombings. Roland Marx [260] published a book in French, Mort d'un amiral: l'IRA contre Mountbatten.

Also published in 1981 was a bizarre work of "historical fiction," George MacBeth [245], The Katana: A Novel Based on the Wartime Diaries of John Beeby. There were 24 untitled chapters and no index. Narrative was in the first person, this "John Beeby" claimed he served under Mountbatten for three years. He described an early assassination attempt in 1944, allegedly by the Japanese, to blow up Mountbatten in Kandy. The narrator claimed he was actually a double-agent, a spy for the British in occupied Singapore. The final implication was that Mountbatten was in fact eventually assassinated, and thus the plot ultimately was a success.

Apparantly not meant to be fiction was the book published in 1990, Richard Deacon [96], pseud.: Donald McCormick, The Greatest Treason: The Bizarre Story of Hollis, Liddell, and Mountbatten. In a shrill concoction, Deacon described an anti-American, pro-Soviet, pro-German, homosexual cabal involving some notorious Britist rogues, Peter Murphy, Peter Wright, Roger Hollis, Guy

Liddell, the Cliveden set, John Vassall, Dr. Armand Hammer, Anthony Blunt, and the notorious trio, Maclean, Burgess, and Philby. The royal family was involved because Mountbatten was a conspirator and a notorious homosexual. The KGB assisted the IRA in assassinating Mountbatten. It goes on and on.

ASSESSMENTS

A lengthy TV documentary was devoted exclusively to Mountbatten. Mountbatten himself assisted in the preparation and did the narration of a major TV documentary shown in thirteen parts in 1966-1967, "The Life and Times of Lord Mountbatten" [237]. Expert advisers were John Terraine and Peter Morley. The Imperial War Museum was an important sponsor. One variation was incorporated in the Twentieth-Century Leaders series.

Mountbatten has been the subject of commemorations, tributes, entries in encyclopedias and dictionaries, documentaries, memorial lectures, and special publications. A recent example was by a close friend, Lord Solly Zuckerman [450], Six Men Out of the Ordinary, foreword by Prince Philip. Six essays were the personal recollections of this great scientific adviser and disarmament expert. Mountbatten (pp. 131-68) was described as "the man of all ambitions. . . . the quintessential admiral, tall, handsome. . . ." He was regarded as a polo-playing playboy, fast cars, travel, and movie stars, but he maintained his professional reputation. Mountbatten himself believed his greatest contribution was the integration of the three armed services under a Secretary of State. Zuckerman candidly discussed the Cecil King affair, a failed effort to oust Prime Minister Wilson.

Reference guides incorporated essays on Mountbatten. The following are samples: Peter Teed [395], Dictionary of Twentieth-Century History, included Mountbatten (p.315); Alan Palmer [317], Dictionary of the British Empire and Commonwealth, included Mountbatten (p. 241); Kenneth Macksey [251], The Penguin Encyclopedia of Military Warfare, included Mountbatten (pp. 223-24); and David Mason [262], Who's Who in World War II, included Mountbatten (207-15).

The Royal United Services Institution established the Mountbatten Memorial Lecture series in 1980. The first lecture was presented by Air Marshal Sir Terrence Lewin [235] at RUSI, London, 7 July 1980 in the presence of Lady Patricia Mountbatten, Lady Pamela Hicks and her husband, David. Lewin recalled the mindless act of terrorism in August 1979. He concluded that an important, if not the most important, contribution of Mountbatten was his initiatives leading to the central organization for defense.

The Dieppe imbroglio continued to plague Mountbatten decades after his death. The Guardian published a special edition commemorating the 50th anniversary of D-Day, Friday, 20 May 1994. Juliet Gardiner [138] contributed an article, "Infamous Rehearsals" (pp. 4-5), recalling OPERATION JUBILEE, a disaster, "the sea equivalent of the Charge of the Light Brigade."

TITLES, HONORS, AND AWARDS

The following are lists of titles and honors applicable to Earl Mountbatten:

--Personal Aide-de-Camp to King Edward VIII
--Personal Aide-de-Camp to King George VI
--Personal Aide-de-Camp to Queen Elizabeth II
--Mentor and Advocate for Prince Philip, Duke of Edinburgh
--"Honorary Grandfather to Charles, Prince of Wales"
--Colonel of the Life Guards
--Colonel Commandant of the Royal Marines
--a series of regimental commands
--Governor of the Isle of Wight
--Lord Lieutenant of the Isle of Wight
--Chairman, Council of the United World Colleges
--Lord Louis Mountbatten (1917)
--first Earl Mountbatten of Burma (1946)
--Baron Romsey of Romsey (1947)
--C.B. (1922) - Companion of the Bath.
--D.S.M. (U.S.) (1945) - Distinguished Service Medal
--D.S.O. (1941) - Distinguished Service Order
--F.R.S. (1966) - Fellow of the Royal Society
--G.C.B. (1955) - Grand Cross of the Bath
--G.C.I.E. (1947) - Knight Grand Commander of the Order of the Star of India
--G.C.S.I. (1947) - Knight Grand Commander of the Indian Empire
--G.V.V.O. (1937) - Knight Grand Cross of the Royal Victorian Order
--K.C.B. (1945) - Knight Commander of the Bath
--K.G. (1946) - Knight of the Garter
--L.M. (1943) - Legion of Merit
--M.V.O. (1920) - Member of the Royal Victorian Order
--O.M. (1965) - Order of Merit
--P.C. (1947) - Privy Council
--Hon. DCL (1946) - Honorary Doctor of Civil Laws, Oxford
--Hon. LLD (1946-1963) - Honorary Doctor of Laws, Cambridge, Leeds, Edinburgh, Southampton, London, Sussex
--Hon. DSc (1948) - Honorary Doctor of Science, Delhi and Patna
--Freeman of the City of London, Edinburgh, and Romsey
--and various Orders from Burma, China, Denmark, Ethiopia, France, Greece, Nepal, Netherlands, Portugal, Rumania, Siam (Thailand), Spain, and Sweden

--"Active member of over 200 organizations" (entry in the <u>Dictionary of National Biography</u> [98] stated 179) For example:

    --All England Lawn Tennis and Croquet Club, Wimbledon
    --Britain-Burma Society
    --British National Electronics Council (founder)
    --Cambridge University Heraldic and Genealogical Society
    --Hampshire County Cricket Club
    --Institution of Naval Architects
    --King George's Fund for Sailors
    --National Electronics Research Council, member and founder
    --Royal Naval Film Corporation
    --Royal Swedish Naval Society
    --Save the <u>VICTORY</u> Fund (father, founder)
    --Sea Scouts, Commodore
    --Society for Nautical Research (patron)
    --United World Colleges, President
    --Zoological Society
    --later, the Mountbatten Memorial Trust
    --the Edwina Mountbatten Trust

Nicknames:
--"Dickie"
--"Uncle Dickie"
--"Tricky Dickie"
--"Superbo" - from "Supremo"
--for "SEAC" - by cynical Americans: "Save England's Asiatic Colonies"
--for "SEAC" - by resentful staff mocking the luxury of the headquarters at Kandy: "Supreme Example of Allied Confusion"

Stilwell used several, not to his face:
--"Glamor Boy"
--"a fatuous ass"
--"childish Louis"
--"publicity crazy"
--and for C-B-I - "Confused Bastards in India"
--together, the Mountbattens were dubbed "the Warrior and the Healer"
--Allied POWs for whom a long time ensued after the Japanese surrender and until they were repatriated: Mountbatten was dubbed "Linger Longer Louis."

Statues and portraits:
--See George Lonn [240], <u>British Portraits: Notable Personalities in Charcoal Sketches</u>, 1984; the front cover was an oil painting of Mountbatten by George Long; charcoal drawings included Prince Philip and Viscount Slim.

--Portrait by John Ulbricht, at the National Portrait Gallery, London
--Portrait by Derek Hill
--The statue of Mountbatten on the Foreign Office Green, London, was sculptured by Frank Belsky [36]. It was unveiled by Queen Elizabeth in November 1983. In her speech, the Queen referred to "Uncle Dickie."

Titles, Honors, and Organizations of Lady Mountbatten. [Noted active association with 100 organizations.]
--Countess Mountbatten of Burma
--Vicereine of India
--C.B.E. (1943) - Commander, Order of the British Empire
--C.I. (1947) - Crown of India
--D.C.V.O. (1946) - Dame Commander of the Royal Victorian Order
--G.B.E. (1947) - Knight Grand Cross, Order of the British Empire
--G.C.St.J. (1945) - Knight Grand Cross, Order of St. John of Jerusalem
--Superintendent-in-Chief, St. John Ambulance Brigade
--President, Royal College of Nurses
--Chair, St. John and Red Cross Services Hospitals
--President, Save the Children Fund
--Red Cross
--Girl Guides

Portraits
--by P.A. de Laszlo at Broadlands
--by Salvador Dali at Broadlands
--by Edward J. Halliday in New Delhi

Addresses of Earl and Countess Mountbatten:
--2 Kinnerton St.
London SW1
and
--Broadlands
Romsey
Hants

FOREWORDS AND INTRODUCTIONS

Note: Following is a list of works for which Earl Mountbaten wrote the foreword or introduction. At the end of each title, the number in brackets is the number of the work listed in Part II, the Annotated Bibliography Section. NOT included in the list are works which are cited in Part I, the Historiographical Narrative Section. The total number of works for which Earl Mountbatten, or, in one case, Lady Mountbatten, wrote forewords or introductions was 52. In addition 13 works, mostly pamphlets and items of limited interest, were found in the Mountbatten personal library located in the Hartley Library of the University of Southampton. Those 13 works are listed separately at the end.

Richard Baker, The Terror of Tobermory, 1972 [21].
George A. Ballard, The Black Battlefleet, 1979 [23].
Derek Beamish, Poole and World War II, 1980 [31].
Patrick Beesly, Very Special Intelligence, 1977 [35].
Barbara Cartland, Book of Useless Information, 1977 [61].
Pamphlet for the Commission for the United World Colleges, 1975 [73].
The Computer Users' Year Book, 1975, 1975 [74].
Malwin Drummond, Salt-water Palaces, 1979 [105].
T.G. Eakins, Hand in Hank, 1970 [110].
Encyclopedia of Sea Warfare, 1975 [116].
Edward Fuller, The Right of the Child, 1951, foreword by Lady Mountbatten [134].
David Harwood, Alert to Danger, 1969 [159].
Cecil Humphery-Smith, ed., The Cambridge Armorial, 1985 [188].
Roy F. Johnson, The Royal George, 1971 [199].
Norman King, All the Queen's Men, 1967 [208].
S.W. Kirby, Singapore, 1971 [209].
Vida Leigh, Mary Bright of Fiddlers Green, 1966 [227].
Kendall McDonald, The Second Underwater Book, 1970 [246].
Leonard Miall, ed., Richard Dimbleby Broadcaster, 1966 [270].
Charles Strong, Common-sense Therapy for Horses' Injuries, 1956 [384].
Charles Strong, Horse Injuries, 1967 [385].
Where Great Adventures Start, 1970 [421].
Clark Worswick, The Last Empire, 1976 [438].
Bruce Wright, The Frogmen of Burma, 1968 [439].

Works not included in Part I, the Annotated Bibliography Section.

Pamphlet for the Charities Aid Foundation.
Variety Club Diary, 1975.
Variety Club Diary, 1976.
Isle of Wight Companion.
Isle of Wight, 1977.
Isle of Wight, 1978.
Isle of Wight Village Book.
Story of Emsworth Sailing Club.
Electronic and Radio Engineering as a Profession.
Interservice Hovercraft Trials Unit.
A Man of Vision: Dr. Rochi Hingorani.

AREAS FOR FUTURE RESEARCH

Earl Mountbatten remains a fascinating and controversial figure. In the Research Guide to European Historical Biography, the author noted "Perhaps only Douglas MacArthur comes close to equalling Mountbatten's many roles and the vigor with which he played them" (III., p. 1452). Having previously (1994) completed a historiographical survey and annotated bibliography on Douglas MacArthur, the author [340] would agree about the similarites of breadth of interest and activities and the extraordinary enthusiasm and diligence of both. There is still much to learn about Mountbatten and about Lady Mountbatten. Much of what we know about the personal lives of each, and their lives together, is still based on rumor. More facts are needed.

With the increasing declassification of sensitive documents, for example about the secret negotiations related to Anglo-American cooperation in the development of nuclear power for propulsion and nuclear weapons such as the Polaris and Trident missiles, more authoritative information will become available about the actual role of Mountbatten in acquiring these systems.

We still do not know exactly what influence Mountbatten had within the royal family. Again, there are many rumors. Why would Prince Charles accuse Mountbatten of being abusive to him? The relationships, Mountbatten, Prince Philip, and Prince Charles must be reevaluated.

The name Mountbatten continues to intrigue us. What was the story about the official "royals" use of Mountbatten-Windsor and/or Windsor. What is the real story of that important matter?

Despite the enormous volume of literature written about the Dieppe raid of 1942, accusations such as those of Brian Villa [412] persist. Yet more research needs to be done to learn the truth. There are obvious gaps in the paper trail, at least Villa is convincing in that regard. Much remains unanswered.

The Cecil King affair of 1968 continues to raise unanswered questions. Mountbatten has been accused of an attempted coup of the Harold Wilson government. What is the truth? More needs to be done to clarify this scandal.

Part II

ANNOTATED BIBLIOGRAPHY

1 Adamthwaite, Anthony. "Suez Revisited." <u>International Affairs</u>, 64 (Summer 1988): 449-64. A revisionist view of the Suez crisis of 1956; instead of the perception that it signified the end of Great Britain as a great power, its impact was surprisingly minor; the Special Relationship was quickly repaired.

2 Akbar, Ahmed. "Jinnah and the Quest for Muslim Indentity." <u>HISTOD</u>, 44 (September 1994): 34-40. Re the founder of Pakistan, Muhammad Ali Jinnah, enigmatic and inscrutible; Akbar, a professor at Cambridge, is preparing a biography; Jinnah is blamed, wrongly Akbar contended, for the failure to unify India.

3 -------. "The Hero in History: Myth, Media and Realities." <u>HISTOD</u>, 46 (March 1996): 7-10. Elaboration on the previous entry; alluding to Thomas Carlyle; an indictment of Mountbatten and Nehru and manipulation of the media so as to depict Jinnah in the worst light: Mountbatten called him a megalomaniac and "a bastard"; examples included the film "Gandhi" and Gopal biography of Nehru; lamentation that the Nehru-Edwina Mountbatten affair which directly influenced events was ignored or glossed over.

4 Albert, J.G. "Attlee, the Chiefs of Staff and the Restructuring of 'Commonwealth Defence' between VJ Day and the Outbreak of the Korean War." Ph.D. diss, Oxford, 1986. The drawdown from World War II and reorganization prior to 1950; this was the structure Mountbatten inherited when he became 1st Sea Lord in 1955; he had been 4th Sea Lord earlier, 1950-1952.

5 Aldgate, Anthony and Richards, Jeffrey. <u>Britain Can Take It: The British Cinema in the Second World War</u>. Edinburgh: UP; NY: Blackwell, 1986, 1994, 312 pp. Cited (pp. 187-217) "In Which We Serve," directed by and starring Noel Coward, as an important example; Coward met Mountbatten and Edwina in July 1941 and was impressed with the story of <u>HMS KELLY</u>; the powerful Beaverbrook, who disliked Coward and Mountbatten, attempted the quash the project.

6   Ali, Chaudri Muhammad. The Emergene of Pakistan. NY: Columbia UP, 1967, 427 pp. A careful and reasoned account of the partition of India presenting the perspective of Pakistan; critical of Gandhi, Nehru, and Mountbatten.

7   Allen, Louis. Burma: The Longest War, 1941-1945. London: Dent; NY: St. Martin, 1984, 1986, 706 pp. An anecdotal but detailed overview of the campaign in Burma by a participant, an intelligence operative, and later, prolific and authoritative analyst; covered operations of British, Indian, Burmese, American, Chinese, and Japanese forces; incorporated Japanese sources; the "longest war" was in two parts: the Japanese drove out the white man (1941-1942) and the white man returned (1944-1945).

8   -------. The End of the War in Asia. London and NY: Beekman, 1976, 1979, 319 pp. A broad, thoughtful analysis of the final months and later consequences of the Asian/Pacific war; emphasis on the Japanese perspective; the Japanese anticipated defeat after the sea blockade and strategic bombing; the problem of Japanese occupation forces throughout the former empire is reviewed; an epilogue described the International Military Tribunal of the Far East, the war crimes trials.

9   -------. "Studies in the Japanese Occupation of South-East Asia." Durham University Journal, 64 (December 1971): 120-32. A review of the Mountbatten Despatches which report on the situation during the last months of the war and first months of peace; complications in Indochina reviewed; General Douglas Gracey was confronted with a chaos; forces with interests included the British, French, American OSS, Chinese, Viet Minh, and the Japanese.

10   -------. "Transfer of Power in Burma: Review Article." JI&CH, 13 (January 1985): 185-94. A review of a Transfer of Power volume, this one on Burma; described the Japanese occupation, the aftermath of the war, the military administration for which Mountbatten was responsible, and Burmese nationalism; Slim, Mountbatten, and Attlee all recognized Aung San as the likely postwar leader; details on disputes between Mountbatten and the Civil Affairs bureaucrats.

11   Allen, Ralph.   Ordeal by Fire: Canada, 1910-1945.   Toronto: Doubleday, 1961, 501 pp. By a Canadian war correspondent; called Dieppe "a magnificent fiasco," a tactical failure but strategic success.

12 Al-Solami, D.A. "British Preparation for the Suez War, 1956." Ph.D. diss, Exeter, 1988. Re the military and political preparations to overthrow Nasser; collaboration with Israel and the secret Sevres Accord; miscalculations and divisions among military and political authorities led to the failure.

13 Aronson, Theo. The Royal Family at War. London: Murray, 1993, 256 pp. Hagiography depicting George VI as "Warrior King"; Mountbatten, a second cousin, was never an official wartime representative of the monarchy, much as he would have desired to be; in February 1945 Mountbatten invited George to visit India but Churchill forbade it, contending the Americans would interpret it as perpetuation of colonialism.

14 Aspinall-Oglander, Cecil F. Roger Keyes: Being a Biography of Admiral of the Fleet Lord Keyes of Zeebrugge and Dover. London: Hogarth, 1951, 494 pp. The authorized biography of the predecessor of Mountbatten as commander of Combined Operations, July 1940-October 1941.

15 Atherton, Louise. SOE Operations in the Far East: An Introductory Guide to the Newly Released Records of the Special Operations Executive in the Public Record Office. London: PRO, 1993, 59 pp. The Waldegrave Initiative of 1992 led to release of new material at the PRO at Kew; included were details of secret SOE operations, for example, with resistance leaders and related to colonial issues upsetting to Americans, not covered in the official histories.

16 Atkin, Ronald. Dieppe 1942: The JUBILEE Disaster. London: Macmillan, 1980, 318 pp. One of the dozens of accounts; use of interviews with survivors and with German participants; blamed Montgomery for selecting the Canadians in the first place.

17 Austin, Alexander B. We Landed at Dawn: The Story of the Dieppe Raid. London and NY: Harcourt Brace; Sydney: Angus, 1943, 1953, 217 pp. An first-hand account by a war correspondent.

18 Azad, Maulana Abul Kalam. India Wins Freedom: An Autobiographical Narrative. Alt. subtitle: The Complete Version. NY and London: Longman, 1959, 1960, 1978, 1988, 317 pp. Introduction by Louis Fischer; dedicated to Nehru; memoir (1888-1958) of an important official of the Congress Party and a Moslem; 30 pages previously suppressed were added to the edition of 1988; chapter (pp. 195-207) on Mountbatten mission; noted extraordinary influence on Nehru of Edwina Mountbatten; critical of position of Gandhi; warned Mountbatten of consequences of partition; all tried to avoid catastrophe but the results were worse than anyone imagined: "When partition took place, rivers of blood flowed" (p. 207).

19   Baker, George E. Mountbatten of Burma. London: Cassell, 1959. A short study of Mountbatten.

20   Baker, Richard. Dry Ginger: The Biography of Admiral of the Fleet Sir Michael Le Fanu. London: Allen, 1977, 254 pp. A biography of Le Fanu (d. 1970), former Chief of Defense Staff and First Sea Lord; the title referred to abolition of the rum ration.

21   -------. The Terror of Tobermory: An Informal Biography of Vice Admiral Sir Gilbert Stephenson. Foreword: Earl Mountbatten. London: Allen, 1972, 196 pp. Stephenson was commander of the Western Isles during the war and was responsible for a rigorous training program for escort warship crews; he was a "terror."

22   Ball, S.J. "Military Nuclear Relations between the U.S. and Great Britain under the Terms of the McMahon Act, 1946-1958." HJ, 38 (June 1995): 439-54. The making of policy of Anglo-American cooperation in the nuclear field ; the U.S. was reluctant because of lapses in British security such as the Fuchs case.

23   Ballard, George A. The Black Battlefleet. Eds.: N.A.M. Rodger and George Osbon. Foreword by Earl Mountbatten. London: Nautical; Annapolis: NIP, 1979, 1980, 261 pp. Folio size with illustrations; reprint of a series of articles in Mariner's Mirror, 1911-1948, by Admiral Ballard, for example, about early battleship design, including the ill-fated HMS CAPTAIN.

24   Barclay, Glen St. John. "'Butcher and Bolt': Admiral Roger Keyes and British Combined Operations, 1940-1941." NWCR, 35 (March 1982): 18-29. Keyes was a veteran of World War I and a favorite of Winston Churchill who appointed him commander of Combined Operations; a series of overly grandiose and failed operations, notably Dakar, resulted in the replacement of Keyes with Mountbatten in October 1941.

25   Barker, A.J. The March on Delhi. London: Faber, 2963, 302 pp. Foreword by Renya Mutaguchi, the former commander of the Japanese 15th Army which attempted to invade India in 1944; an account of that campaign and its aftermath; reviewed the Allied command structure including the formation of SEAC after the Quebec Conference; the Mutaguchi-Barker correspondence which included criticism of another Japanese general caused a stir in Japan.

26   --------. Suez: The Seven Day War. NY: Praeger; London: Faber, 1964, 1965, 223 pp. An hour-by-hour account of the crisis by a British Army officer-historian.

27   Barnett, Correlli. Engage the Enemy More Closely: The Royal Navy in the Second World War. NY: Norton; London: Hodder, 1991, 1072 pp. By the director of the Churchill archives center at Cambridge University; praised as model of "total history" approach; the title is from Lord Nelson's last signal at Trafalgar; an operational history of the Royal Navy which functioned creditably and effectively especially in defeating the U-boat threat and in the Normandy invasion; Mountbatten as Combined Operations commander, Dieppe raid, early planning for Normandy, and a SEAC commander covered (pp. 540-555, 756-80, 865-72).

28   Barratt, John and Ritchie, Jean. With the Greatest Respect: The Private Lives of Earl Mountbatten and Prince and Princess Michael of Kent. London: Sidgwick, 1991, 234 pp. A memoir by the private secretary of Mountbatten; enlightening on day-to-day activities.

29   Barris, Ted and Barris, Alex. Days of Victory: Canadians Remember, 1939-1945. Toronto: Macmillan, 1995, 1996, 312 pp. Canadians "came of age" and Dieppe was "the bloodiest nine hours in the Second World War"; 5000 Canadians seen as "sacrificial lambs" (pp. vi, 19-26); shrill and anti-Mountbatten and anti-British throughout.

30   Bartlett, Merrill L., ed. Assault from the Sea: Essays on the History of Amphibious Warfare. London: Arms; Annapolis: NIP, 1983, 473 pp. A series of essays by experts on modern amphibious warfare; included account of Dieppe and preparations for Normandy (pp. 249-60, 308-19).

31   Beamish, Derek, et al. Poole and World War II. Foreword by Earl Mountbatten. Poole, Eng: Historical Trust, 1980, 239 pp. Described the variety of participation in the war associated with Poole, a coastal city in the south of England.

32   Beaufre, Andre. The Suez Expedition, 1956. London: Faber; NY: Praeger, 1967, 1969, 161 pp. Trans: Richard Barry; by a French army commander; re the planning process; critical of British efforts.

33   Beaumont, Roger A. Military Elites: Special Fighting Units in the Modern World. Indianapolis: Bobbs, 1974, 265 pp. A general survey of some of the more prominent units, e.g., Merrill's Marauders, the Rangers, and Green

Berets; credited Mountbatten with the creation of some of the early units for raids (pp. 48-51).

34 --------. Special Operations and Elite Units, 1939-1988: A Research Guide. Research Guides in Military History series. Westport, CT: Greenwood, 1988, 258 pp. An extensive reference guide including sources about combined operations, commandos, and other elite units; Mountbatten oversaw formation and operations of these types of forces.

35 Beesly, Patrick. Very Special Intelligence: The Story of the Admiralty's Operational Intelligence Centre, 1939-1945. Foreword by Earl Mountbatten. London: Hamilton; NY: Doubleday, 1978, 307 pp. By a prominent expert on intelligence matters; how naval intelligence operations assisted in winning the war, especially in Europe.

36 Belsky, Frank. Statue of Earl Mountbatten, Foreign Office Green, Whitehall, London, unveiled November 1983. Belsky was the sculptor, unveiled by Queen Elizabeth II.

37 Bidwell, Shelford. The Chindit War: Stilwell, Wingate, and the Campaign in Burma, 1944. NY: Macmillan, 1979, 1980, 304 pp. Introduction by John Masters; Wingate and Chindit operations became controversial and Stilwell was a notorious Anglophobe, calling Mountbatten "Glamor Boy"; Mountbatten was overall commander; elaboration of two types of warfare which differed significantly, that of Wingate and that of Stilwell.

38 Bond, Brian, ed. Chief of Staff: The Diaries of Lt.-General Sir Henry Pownall. 2 vols. Hamden: Archon, 1973-1974, 615 pp. Pownall was Chief of Staff, SEAC, under Mountbatton; the rationale of his appointment: Pownall was a "wise old hand" who would act as a steadying influence on the inexperienced and perhaps overimpulsive young Mountbatten; his health declined and he returned home late in 1944.

39 Boothroyd, Basil. Prince Philip: An Informal Biography. London: Longman; NY: McCall, 1971, 238 pp. A biography of Philip, protege of Mountbatten; a semi-official study.

40 Bradford, Sarah. King George VI. Alt. title: The Reluctant King. NY: St. Martin; London: Weidenfeld, 1989, 1990, 520 pp. By an aide to the royal family; more details about the Duke and Duchess of Windsor; the abdication of the former led to succession of George, 1895-1952; covered the career of "Dickie" Mountbatten.

41 Brecher, Michael. Nehru: A Political Biography. NY: Oxford UP, 1959, 1960, 682 pp. and abridged, 1966, 267 pp. A standard biography of Nehru, 1889-1964, the most important figure during the period of the Viceroyalty of Mountbatten, independence, and partition

42 Brewer, James F., et al., eds. China Airlift-The Hump: China's Aerial Lifeline, the Beginning of the China-Burma-India Hump Pilots Association. 2 vols. Popular Bluff, MO: Association, 1980-1983, 1224 pp. Dedicated to Mountbatten; large folio size with colored illustrations; veterans of the massive air supply effort, India and Burma to China formed the association in 1946; annual meetings, e.g., 1981 in Milwaukee; mini-biography of "Lord Louis [sic] Mountbatten" (I, p. 510).

43 Broadbent, Sir Ewen. The Military and Government: From Macmillan to Heseltine. NY: St. Martin, 1988, 251 pp. Foreword by Harold Macmillan; Mountbatten figured in many aspects: the White Paper of 1946 calling for unification and a unified ministry, service as Chief of Staff, and unification of the services during the Healey period.

44 Broadlands Archives. Catalogues and Guides to the Archives. Southampton: USH Library, 1991. Loose-leaf notebook, an "interim catalogue"; a summary listing of the papers of Edwina Mountbatten, Prince Louis of Battenberg, Sir Edward Cassel, and Mountbatten, among others; the Mountbatten papers; a description of the Mountbatten library, e.g., a listing of books by Mountbatten and books with forewords by Mountbatten; under the control of the Trustees who sponsored the official biography by Ziegler.

45 Brookshire, Jerry H. Clement Attlee. Manchester, England: UP, 1995, 1996, 269 pp. A recent scholarly biography of Attlee, 1883-1967; Mountbatten figures prominently at the time of the transfer of power in India.

46 Brown, David. "Mountbatten as First Sea Lord." JRUSI, 131 (June 1986): 63-68. By the head of the Naval History Branch; an assessment of the accomplishments of Mountbatten as professional head of the Royal Navy during a crucial time of entrenchment; disagrees with Ziegler, the official biographer, e.g., Mountbatten was well received in the navy and that it performed well during the Suez operations in 1956.

47 Brown, Judith M. Modern India: The Origins of an Asian Democracy. Short Oxford History of the Modern World. NY: Oxford UP, 1985, 1994, 480 pp. A standard survey of modern India; places the war, negotiations toward independence, and the transfer in perspcetive; informative on the significant and controversial Cripps Mission and "interference" by FDR; Wavell blamed the failure to unify on "three old men": Gandhi, Jinnah, and Churchill.

48   Bryant, Sir Arthur. A History of the War Years Based on the Diaries of Field Marshal Lord Alanbrooke, Chief of the Imperial General Staff. 2 vols. NY: Doubleday; London: Collins, 1957-1959, 1113 pp. Foreword by Lord Alanbrooke; from autobiographical notes of the most important military advisor to Churchill, present at the summit conferences including second Quebec when Mountbatten was appointed SAC SEAC; some claim Bryant tampered with the diaries and the originals at the Liddell Hart Center should be consulted.

49   Buckley, Christoper. Norway, the Commandos, Dieppe. The Second World War, 1939-1945: A Short Military History series. London: HMSO, 1952, 1977. A popular, quasi-official account of some early campaigns by a war correspondent and reprinted 25 years later; originally, the Directorate of Raiding Operations was formed in June 1940; commandos created; Keyes made Director; later in October 1941, Mountbatten made Director; extensive coverage of Dieppe (pp. 227-70).

50   Burke, Samuel M. and Al Din Quraishi, Salim. The British Raj in India: A Historical Review. NY: Oxford UP, 1995, 600 pp. A recent scholarly study with global perspectives, including the crucial transfer of power.

51   Burke's Guide to the Royal Family. Burke's Genealogical series. Foreword by Earl Mountbatten. London: Burke, 1973, 374 pp. Mountbatten noted he had lived through six reigns including that of Victoria; she held Mountbatten at christening; George V abandoned all German styles and titles during World War I and took the "Windsor" name; biographies of the monarchs.

52   Butler, David. Lord Mountbatten: The Last Viceroy. London: Methuen, 1985, 343 pp. 15 untitled chapters; touted as a "novel" which was made into a TV mini-series, a George Walker Television Production starring Nicol Williamson as Mountbatten.

53   Callahan, Raymond A. Burma, 1942-1945. The Politics and Strategy of the Second World War. London: Poynter; Newark: U Delaware P, 1978, 1979, 190 pp. A history of the second Burma campaign which culminated in the defeat of the Japanese forces; details of the Mountbatten command, e.g., being forced to contend with decreasing resources and manpower plus additional territory added to SEAC from SWPac; emphasis on political factors and inner-allied relations.

54   Calvert, Michael. Slim. Ballantine Illustrated History: War Leader series # 12. NY: Ballantine, 1973, 160 pp. Introduction by A.J. Barker; a short popular biography by a participant in the Burma campaign.

55   Campbell, John P. Dieppe Revisited: A Documentary Investigation. Studies in Intelligence series. Portland, OR: Cass, 1993, 1995, 263 pp. By a professor at McMaster University; use of Allied and German sources; claim that more is published about Dieppe than D-Day; reaffirmed the traditional interpretations: that there were no intelligence leaks (David Irving, Anthony Cave Brown, and Brian Villa claimed otherwise), German radar failed to detect the invasion force, and expose about other legends associated with Dieppe; 48 German aircraft destroyed and 106 Allied aircraft; much debate over "lessons learned" from Dieppe.

56   Campbell-Johnson, Alan. Mission with Mountbatten. Foreword by Earl Mountbatten. London: Jarrolds; NY: Dutton, 1951, 1953, 1961, 1972. 370 pp. By the press attache on the staff of Mountbatten as Viceroy; an "inside" account of the transfer of power.

57   Canella, Charles J. "Study in Combined Command: C-B-I." MILREV, 45 (July 1965): 55-71. An extensive analysis of the complexities of the command structure of SEAC; it demonstrated inadequate strategic guidance and poorly designed apparatus; there were five separate headquarters; Stilwell's position was impossible; a dispute led to the recall of the British naval commander.

58   Cannadine, David. The Pleasures of the Past. London: Collins; NY: Norton, 1989, 1995, 348 pp. A collection of book reviews, many on the monarchy of Great Britain; Edward VII was a "selfish simpleton" and Mountbatten was the first of "many morticians of Empire."

59   Canning, John, ed. 100 Great Modern Lives: Makers of the World Today from Faraday to Kennedy. London: Odhams, 1965, 1967, 640 pp. Included "Louis Mountbatten" (pp. 594-99); getting HMS KELLY ready for war.

60   Carter, April.   Mahatma Gandhi: A Selected Bibliography. Bibliographies of World Leaders series # 2. Westport, CT: Greenwood, 1995, 177 pp. Five citations from the index on Mountbatten; Ziegler biography included.

61   Cartland, Barbara. Book of Useless Information: In Aid of the United World Colleges. Foreword by Earl Mountbatten. London: Transworld, 1977, 128 pp. By the prolific author, friend, and patron of United World Colleges, Mountbatten's charity; Cartland called the contents "brain litter."

62   -------. Love at the Helm: Inspired and Helped by Earl Mountbatten of Burma. London: Weidenfeld; London: Magna, 1980, 1981, 272 pp. A memorial tribute to Mountbatten; he had assisted her in the naval background of many of her novels; proceeds of some novels went to the St. John Ambulance Brigade; proceeds from this book to go to the Mountbatten Memorial Trust.

63   Carver, Michael. Twentieth-Century Warriors: The Development of the Armed Forces of Major Military Nations in the Twentiery Century. NY: Weidenfeld, 1987, 1988, 478 pp. By Field Marshal Lord Carver, Chief of the Defence Staff; a review of how military powers have adjusted to technological advances; gave credit to Mountbatten first as Chief of Combined Operations and later as Chief of the Defense Staff for integration, cooperation, and coordination of the armed forces of Great Britain; the results were even felt in the Falklands/Malvinas campaign long after Mountbatten was dead.

64   -------, ed. The War Lords: Military Commanders in the Twentieth Century. Boston: Little, Brown; London: Weidenfeld, 1976, 640 pp. Short biographies of 43 commanders, three from the Royal Navy; included Mountbatten, the essay by Ronald Brockman (pp. 357-74).

65   Castle, Charles. Noel. London: Allen; NY: Doubleday, 1972, 1973, 272 pp. Re Noel Coward; an account of the making of "In Which We Serve"; Castle interviewed Mountbatten (pp. 173-76); they had met in 1924 and Coward visited Mountbatten's ships periodically; Coward adapted the story of HMS KELLY; Mountbatten put pressure on the Ministry of Information to give approval.

66   Chakkar: The Magazine of Polo around the World. A Magazine, 1986, 128 pp. Folio-size; included an article, "The Spectator at Polo," by "Marco" (pp. 44-50), the nom de plume of Mountbatten.

67   Chakkar: Polo around the World. Ed. by Herbert Spencer. Essays by Mountbatten, the Duke of Edinburgh, and Baron Elie de Rothschild; Chakkar is an Indian word for "chukker," a period of play in Polo.

68   Charmley, John. Churchill's Grand Alliance: The Anglo-American Special Relationship, 1940-1957. London: Hodder, 1995, 443 pp. By the noted revisionist on Winston Churchill; this on the role of Churchill and the Special Relationship; Mountbatten gained increasing responsibility and influence on these matters during this time, e.g., Mountbatten questioned Prime Minister Eden about the consequences of the Suez campaign and Eden changed the subject (p. 322).

69   Clifford, Kenneth J. Amphibious Warfare Development in Britain and America, 1920-1940. Laurens, NY: Edgewood, 1983, 312 pp. Development of amphibious warfare was a priority in both countries and significant advances were made; utilized by Combined Operations.

70   Collins, Larry and Lapierre, Dominique. Freedom at Midnight. NY: Simon & Schuster; NY: Avon, 1975, 1976, 572 pp. A popular account with long descriptions of the horrors of communal violence concerning the transfer of power and the division of India; superficial; exaggerated the role of Mountbatten; included 15 interviews with Mountbatten, the transcripts of which are in the Broadlands Archive at Southampton.

71   -------. Mountbatten and Independent India, 16 August 1947-18 June 1948. New Delhi: Tarang, 1982, 1985, 309 pp. From a series of 15 personal interviews with Mountbatten; included official reports by Mountbatten as Governor-General of India after independence.

72   Combined Operations: The Official Story of the Commandos. Foreword by Earl Mountbatten. NY: Macmillan, 1943, 168 pp. By Hilary Aiden St. George Saunders; accounts of some early operations, including Dieppe.

73   Commission for the United World Colleges. Foreword by Earl Mountbatten. Princeton: Xerox, [1975], 16 pp. A pamphlet describing the colleges; Mountbatten was President of the International Council, UWC.

74   The Computer Users' Year Book, 1975. Foreword by Earl Mountbatten. Brighton: Grange, 1975, 860 pp. Mountbatten founded the National Electronics Council in 1964; much service rendered by the Council.

75   Connell, Brian. Manifest Destiny: A Study in Five Profiles of the Rise and Influence of the Mountbatten Family. London: Cassell, 1953, 226 pp. A family chronicle including Prince Louis of Battenburg, Earl Mountbatten, and Prince Philip plus Sir Ernest Cassell and Lady Mountbatten.

76   Connell, G.G. Mediterranean Maelstrom: HMS JERVIS and the Fourteenth Flotilla. London: Kimber, 1987, 272 pp. There were 16 "J" and "K" class destroyers and only 4 survived; most operated in the Mediterranean; Jervis was a sister-ship of Kelly and received 13 battle stars.

77   Controvich, James T. The Central Pacific Campaign, 1943-1944: A Bibliography. Bibliographies of Battles and Leaders series # 2. Westport: Meckler, 1990, 152 pp. A historiographical survey with 1128 briefly annotated entries about the most important period of one of the three major theaters of the Asian/Pacific war, the other two being the Southwest Pacific and C-B-I.

78   Cookbridge, E.H. Die Battenbergs: Geschichte einer Europaischen Familie. Munchen: Biederstein, 1967, 248 pp. A history of the Battenberg, later Mountbatten, family in German; chapters VIII. and IX.   Der Oberbefehlshaber and Die Erbin (pp. 148-91) on Earl and Lady Mountbatten.

79   -------. From Battenbert to Mountbatten. NY: John Day, 1966, 1968, 323 pp. The Battenberg name was created in 1851, originally Hesse, tracing its ancestry back to Charlemagne; by 1917, because of rising anti-German feeling it was changed to Mountbatten.

80   Copland, Ian. "Lord Mountbatten and the Integration of the Indian States: A Reappraisal." JI&CH, 21 (May 1993): 385-408. A focus on a special case in the transfer of power, the Indian princely states; H.D. Hodson and ("astonishing") Philip Ziegler assessed the role of Mountbatten "a personal triumph"; Copland concluded the role of Mountbatten was less impressive: he abandoned the princes in favor of support of the Congress Party.

81   Corfield, Sir Conrad. The Princely India I Knew: From Reading to Mountbatten. London: Indo-British, 1975. A memoir recalling the regimes of several Viceroys.

82   Coultass, Clive. "The Battle of the River Plate." HISTOD, 46 (August 1996): 23-28. Re the making of film in the 1950s about this brilliant victory of the Royal Navy and British diplomats of Latin America against the German Pocket Battleship GRAF SPEE, forced to scuttle; Mountbatten supported the film as a demonstration of a naval battle "on gentlemenly terms" and patriotism.

83   Coupland, Reginald. The Cripps Mission. Oxford: UP, 1942, 91 pp. A contemporaneous account of an important negotiation between the British government and leaders of the Indian Congress Party; the mission was headed by Sir Richard Stafford Cripps (1889-1952).

84   -------. The Indian Problem: Report on the Constitutional Problem in India. 3 vols. in 1. NY: Oxford UP, 1944, 711 pp. A quasi-official analysis of the background for the transfer of power.

85   Coward, Noel. Noel Coward: Autobiography. London: Methuen; London: Heinemann; NY: Doubleday, 1937, 1954, 1986, 526 pp. A new edition, formerly three volumes, of the memoir of Coward, (1899-1973); numerous references to the Mountbattens, e.g., at a dinner Mountbatten told Coward of the sinking of HMS KELLY off Crete; this led to Coward initiating the project which culminated in "In Which We Serve";   Coward was a controversial figure and there were obstacles; Mountbatten intervened to remove most.

86   -------. The Noel Coward Diaries. Boston: Little Brown, 1982, 698 pp. Ed. by Graham Payn and Sheridan Morley; publication of the diaries of Coward, a close friend of the Mountbattens.

87   Cras, Herve. Dieppe: The Dawn of Decision. London: Souvenir, 1962, 1963, 285 pp. Pseud.: Jacques Mordal; a description in detail of the preparation and execution of the raid; explanation of why Dieppe and the Canadians were selected.

88   Cross, John P. Red Jungle. Foreword by Earl Mountbatten. London: Hale, 1957, 244 pp. A personal memoir by a British soldier, a member of the "stay-behind" forces during the Japanese occupation of Malaya; ultimately rescued by submarine.

89   Crowe, William J. "The Policy Roots of the Modern Royal Navy, 1946-1963."   Ph.D. diss. Princeton, 1965, 467 pp.   Coincides with the period Mountbatten led the navy and the services; the role of the Royal Navy was established in the 1890s but was transformed, and much diminished, after World War II; in the search for alternatives the result was the Polaris missile which meant revival of the central role of the navy.

90   Darby, Phillip G.C. British Defence Policy East of Suez, 1947-1968. London: Oxford UP, 1973, 382 pp. Re "the long recessional" of the British empire; earlier the dominance of the Indian Ocean by the Royal Navy was essential and was maintained; by the late 1960s economic realtities forced retreat east of Suez; the withdrawal was "more humane and elegant" than that of others, e.g., the U.S. from Vietnam.

91   -------. "British Defence Policy in the Indian Ocean Region between the Indian Independence Act, 1947, and the British Defence Review, 1966." Ph.D. diss., Oxford, 1969. A dissertation which was the basis for the previous entry.

92   Darwin, John. Britain and Decolonisation. Making of the Twentieth Century series. NY: St. Martin, 1988, 391 pp. From an outstanding series; a chronological survey combining coverage of the old empire, e.g., Canada and Australia, other colonies, e.g., India and African states, and informal empire, e.g., Iran and Egypt; concluded Great Britain decolonized with grace, not as "weary titan."

93   Das, Manmath Nath. Partition and Independence of India: Inside Story of the Mountbatten Days. New Delhi: Vision, 1982, 344 pp. A critical review with revisionist conclusions of the 145 days of the Mountbatten Viceroyalty; the results were almost incomprehesible chaos of events; speculated about the behind-the-scenes roles of obstruction of Churchill and Jinnah, e.g., Churchill wanted Gandhi dead.

94   Davie, Michael, ed. The Diaries of Evelyn Waugh. London: Weidenfeld; Boston: Little Brown, 1976, 824 pp. Another instance of celebrities as friends with the Mountbattens.

95   Davies, John P., Jr. Dragon by the Tail: American, British, Japanese, and Russian Encounters with China and with One Another. NY: Norton, 1972, 448 pp. By the noted "China Hand"; a diplomatic survey of modern Chinese history and international relations; discussion of the creation of SEAC and conflicts among the key personalities, e.g., Chiang, Chennault, Stilwell, and Mountbatten; later strained relations between Mountbatten and Stilwell over the "lunatic chain of command" (pp. 269-311).

96   Deacon, Richard. The Greatest Treason: The Bizarre Story of Hollis, Liddell and Mountbatten. London: Century, 1989, 1990, 224 pp. Pseud.: Donald McCormick; a series of extreme and unsubstantiated claims associated with some known British spies who were, on occasion, pro-German, pro-Soviet, traitors, and homosexuals: Burgess, Maclean, Philby, Blunt, etc.; these accusations included members of the royal family, e.g., Mountbatten, who was homosexual, Deacon contended, part of the Clivedon set, and pro-Communist; he influenced the Prince of Wales; noted some claim Mountbatten was assassinated by American agents, not the IRA; others claim the KGB helped the IRA.

97   Dennis, Peter. Troubled Days of Peace: Mountbatten and the South East Asia Command, 1945-1946. War, Armed Forces and Society series. Manchester: UP; NY: St. Martin, 1987, 281 pp. By an Australian historian trained in the U.S.; focused on the immediate postwar situation; the Japanese surrender was premature, the Allies were exhausted and ill-prepared to deal with massive problems, the Japanese had purposely assisted and encouraged nationalist movements, and the Americans, anti-colonialists, encouraged them, further complicating the situation; Mountbatten called them "troubled days of peace"; without consulting Mountbatten the Allied authorities added one and a half million square miles more territory to SEAC; Admiral King and Stilwell were notorious Anglophobes; Dennis documented misguided and short-sighted policies of the U.S.; as for Mountbatten, history will judge him harshly, e.g., because of his personal vanity and ambition, but, at least, he saw the problems more clearly.

98   Dictionary of National Biography. Over 30 vols. London: Oxford UP, 1885-1993. The standard biographical dictionary of the British, a completely new edition is projected for 2004; see the "Mountbatten" entry.

99   "Dieppe 1942." After the Battle, 5 (n.m. 1974): 1-27. A brief survey of Operation JUBILEE, the planning, the execution, and a description with photos of Dieppe in 1974.

100   Dimbleby, Jonathan. The Prince of Wales: A Biography. London: Little Brown, 1994, 1995, 620 pp. By a broadcast journalist; the official biography with access to diaries and other papers; details on breakdown of the marriage and admission of affair with Camilla Parker-Bowles; blames Prince Philip and Mountbatten for abusing him and making his life miserable.

101   Donnison, F.S.V., ed. British Military Administration in the Far East, 1943-1946. History of the Second World War. London: HMSO, 1956, 500 pp. By a British civil servant; a volume in the Official History of the war; concerned the military adinistration of occupied territories such as Burma, Malaya, and Indochina, e.g., the mission of General Gracey and a British force to assume authority and the return of the French colonial regime.

102   Dooley, Howard J. "Great Britain's 'Last Battle' in the Middle East: Notes on Cabinet Planning during the Suez Crisis of 1956." IHR, 11 August 1989): 486-517. After the 30-year rule, Cabinet records were released; a description and analysis of the Anglo-French planning and response during 1956 associated with the Suez crisis.

103   Dorril, Stephen and Ramsay, Robin. Smear: Wilson and the Secret State. London: Fourth Estate, 1991, 416 pp. More and more has come out about various plots to overthrow the Labor government of Harold Wilson during the 1960s; this account focused on the Cecil King Affair; on 8 May 1968, King and Mountbatten met and discussed the possibility of overthrowing Wilson, to be replaced by Mountbatten as head of a coalition government; Lord Solly Zuckerman showed concern and the meeting ended; Ziegler claimed Mountbatten envisioned only constitutional processes.

104   Douglas, W.A.B. and Greenhous, Brereton. Out of the Shadows: Canada and the Second World War. NY: Oxford UP, 1977, 288 pp. An overview of Canada and Canadian operations in the war; included were accounts of Dieppe and Hong Kong, both debacles where Canadian forces experienced inordinate numbers of casualties.

105   Drummond, Malden. Salt-water Palaces. Introduction by Earl Mountbatten. London, 1979. A popular history of yachting; Mountbatten's introduction was completed only a few days before his assassination.

106   Dunn, Peter M. The First Vietnam War. London: Hurst, NY: St. Martin, 1985, 408 pp. A history from the British perspective of the period of transition from the Japanese occupation and surrender, the arrival of General Gracey and the British force, and the ultimate restoration of the French colonial regime; apologetics for Gracey and critical of the naivete of the U.S.; claimed the U.S. placed obstacles in the way of a British, then a French, return and provided encouragement and assistance to Ho Chi Minh and the Viet Minh; wherever the Amerians prevailed all became Communist whereas wherever Great Britain was in control all remained anti-Communist, e.g., Malaya, Thailand, and Singapore.

107   -------. "OPERATION MASTERDOM: The British in Vietnam, 1945-1946." Ph.D. diss., Nevada, 1973. A dissertation on which the preceding entry was based.

108   Dupuy, Trevor N., et al., eds. The Harper Encyclopedia of Military Biography: From 3500 to the Present. NY: HarperCollins, 1992, 1993, 1216 pp. A reference encyclopedia with 3000 entries on military leaders; the Mountbatten entry (pp. 527-528) was by David Bongard.

109   Durnford-Slater, John. Commando: Memoirs of a Fighting Commando in World War II. London: Kimber; Annapolis: NIP, 1953, 1991. Memoir by an army Brigadier, a participant with the early commandos which evolved into

SAS and SBS; veteran of the Keyes regime and of Dieppe; in the later investigation of Dieppe, concluded that there was no hint that the Germans had been warned.

110   Eakins, T.G. Hand in Hank. Foreword by Earl Mountbatten. Belfast: Baird, 1970, 103 pp. A short book about the Variety Club of Ireland, a children's charity involving a rehabilitation and training center.

111   Eden, Anthony, Earl of Avon. The Memoirs of Anthony Eden, Earl of Avon. 3 vols. London: Cassell; Boston: Houghton, 1960-1965, 2126 pp. Apologetics in this extensive series of recollections; Eden was Foreign Minister under Churchill and later Prime Minister when Mountbatten was 1st Sea Lord, espcially during the Suez crisis, for which Eden was blamed, and he soon left office.

112   Edwardes, Michael. The Last Years of British India. London and Cleveland: World, 1963, 256 pp. An "essay in explanation" of events associated with the transfer of power, espcially as it affected Great Britain, India, and Pakistan; the Labor government hailed it, the Conservatives screamed treachery, and other colonial powers denounced it; much on the role of Mountbatten.

113   -------. Nehru: A Political Biography. NY: Praeger, 1971, 351 pp. A biography of Nehru; covered the role of Mountbatten in the transfer of power.

114   Eiler, Keith E., ed. Wedemeyer on War and Peace. Stanford: Hoover, 1987, 267 pp. Foreword by John Keegan; selected documents and commentary on the Albert C. Wedemeyer (1896-1989) papers held at the Hoover Institution; a ubiquitious and influential American general, formulator of the "victory plan" for World War II and replacement for Stilwell in the SEAC and as Chief of Staff to Chiang; a chapter on the war in Southeast Asia (pp. 67-79).

115   The Empire Club of Canada. Addresses, 1967-1968. Ontario: Don Mills, 1968, 488 pp. A series of published speeches made to the Empire Club; on 11 July 1967 at the Centennial Dinner, Earl Mountbatten spoke, "The Unsinkable Commonwealth"; other speakers included Richard Nixon and Edward Heath.

116   Encyclopedia of Sea Warfare: From the First Ironclad to the Present Day. Salamander Book. Foreword by Earl Mountbatten. London: Spring, 1975, 260 pp. Ed. by Lain Parsons; Mountbatten's foreword is a personal recollection of his early service, joining HMS LION, Admiral Beatty's flagship, seven weeks after the battle of Jutland, and of the operations of HMS KELLY;

the encyclopedia consisted of a series of essays by noted naval historians, e.g., Oliver Warner, Donald Macintyre, and Antony Preston.

117   Evans, Sir Geoffrey C. Slim as Military Commander. Military Commander series. London: Batsford; Princeton: Van Nostrand, 1969, 239 pp. By a division commander under Field Marshal Sir William Slim, the brilliant and successful commander of the 14th Army during the Burma campaign; Mountbatten, who assisted the author, called Slim the best general of the World War II.

118   Evans, William. My Mountbatten Years: In the Service of Lord Louis. London: Headline, 1989, 182 pp. By a staff person who served Mountbatten for a decade; much detail on the family tree, titles, honors, decorations, charities, organizations, places he slept, and uniforms.

119   Fairbanks, Douglas, Jr. The Fairbanks Album: Drawn from the Family Archives. Boston: Graphic Society, 1975, 287 pp. Foreword by Douglas Fairbanks, Jr., narrative by Richard Schibel; folio size with many illustrations including several of Mountbatten.

120   -------. A Hell of a War. NY: St. Martin, 1993, 278 pp. Sequel to Salad Days; the memoir of World War II by Fairbanks (b. 1909); dedicated to the memory of Mountbatten, "hero and friend and honorary God-father of my three Graces, Daphne, Victoria, and Melissa. . . ." Fairbanks, an officer in the U.S. Navy, served on the staff of Combined Operations under Mountbatten; Fairbanks claimed Mountbatten opposed the frontal attack tactic and actually opposed Dieppe as a target but was overruled; recalled one of the lovers of Lady Mountbatten, Bunny Phillips.

121   -------. Salad Days. London: Collins, 1988, 445 pp. Memoir of this famous film star and close friend to the Mountbattens who exchanged visits in Hollywood, New York City, London, and Broadlands.

122   Faligot, Roger. Nous avons tue Mountbatten!: L'IRA parle. Paris: Jean Picollec, 1981, 227 pp. A French work featuring interviews with an IRA commander and details of his role in the assassination of Mountbatten in 1979; additional details on imprisonment and a series of hunger strikes in 1981.

123   Fay, Peter Ward. The Forgotten Army: India's Armed Struggle for Independence, 1942-1945. Ann Arbor: UMichP; Estover: Plybridge, 1993, 1994, 1996, 583 pp. The standard history of the neglected Indian National Army and its commander, Subhas Chandra Bose, India's "lost fuehrer," now seen as a hero in India but as anathma by the British; the INA conducted an unsuccessful campaign with the Japanese against the British in Burma, aimed at invasion of Inda; an informative historiographical essay on sources.

124   Fergusson, Sir Bernard E. The Watery Maze: The Story of Combined Operations. London: Collins; New York: Holt, Rinehart, 1961, 445 pp. Later Lord Ballantrae (b. 1911), a veteran commander in the Burma campaign; a general survey of the development of amphibious warfare in Great Britain by an insider; Keyes was the first director, later replaced by Mountbatten; the Dieppe raid recounted.

125   -------. "The Wingate 'Myth': Review Article." JRUSI, 117 (September 1972): 75-76. A part of the extensive debate over Orde Wingate, for and against; Fergusson has been criticized for attacking the reputation of Wingate, indeed, in a personal letter, Michael Carver accused him of betrayal, "denying him thrice."

126   Fischer, Edward. The Chancy War: Winning in China, Burma, and India in World War II. NY: Orion, 1991, 256 pp. Thirteen untitled chapters and an epilogue about the C-B-I theater, the least chronicled of all in the war; a "chancy war" which meant "if you ask for supplies, a chance you may get them, a greater chance you won't."

127   Fisher, Clive. Noel Coward. NY: St. Martin; London: Weidenfeld, 1992, 301 pp. A recent biography of Coward with coverage of the making of the movie about Mountbatten and HMS KELLY, a later tour of Burma, and the fact of homosexuality of Coward; Lord Beaverbrook and the mass media opposed "In Which We Serve"; Coward retaliated in the opening scene, showing the Daily Express with a ridiculous headline.

128   Fjellman, Margit. Louise Mountbatten, Queen of Sweden. London, 1965, 1968, 232 pp. The daughter of Prince and Princess Battenberg and sister of Mountbatten became Queen of Sweden (d. 1965); details of family relations.

129   Flamini, Roland. Sovereign: Elizabeth II and the Windson Dynasty. NY: Delacorte, 1991, 440 pp. A biography of the Queen and the story of the family name; many references to "Dickie"; an account of the effort to have the dynasty name changed from Windsor to Mountbatten (pp. 245-48).

130   Florence, Arnold. Queen Victoria at Osborne. Foreword by Earl Mountbatten. London: Yelf; London: English Heritage, 1977, 1987, 100 pp. Mountbatton, Governor and Lord Lieutenant of the Isle of Wight; an account of

the visits of Queen Victoria to the Isle of Wight in the nineteenth century; the
Mountbatten family lived at Osborne House, 1914-1921.

131   Foot, M.R.D. "Dieppe: Triumph Out of Disaster: Cross Current."
HISTOD, 42 (August 1992): 10-11. On the occasion of the 50th anniversary,
an assessment of the debate and controversy about OPERATION RUTTER,
cancelled, then reactivated as OPERATION JUBILEE, the disastrous raid on the
French port of Dieppe on 19 August 1942; "much rubbish" has appeared about
it; the Beaverbrook, formerly pro-Mountbatten, turned savagely against him;
noted the Germans were not forewarned.

132   Forester, Cecil Scott. [Mountbatten]. Not published. Forester, the
prolific naval novelist and historian was to be the official biographer of
Mountbatten; upon his death in 1966, Philip Ziegler took over the project.

133   Franks, Norman L.R. The Greatest Air Battle: Dieppe, 19th August
1942. London: Kimber, 1979, 1992, 256 pp. An hour-by-hour account of the
RAF air operations during the raid on Dieppe, a total of 16 hours; 3000 sorties
and 71 squadrons participated; claimed this RAF vs. Luftwaffe operation was
"the greatest air battle of the war."

134   Fuller, Edward. The Right of the Child: A Chapter in Social History.
Foreword by Lady Mountbatten. London: Gollancz, 1951, 159 pp. Intro. by
L.H. Green; the story of the Save the Children Fund, Lady Mountbatten,
president.

135   Fullick, Roy and Powell, Geoffrey. Suez: The Double War. London:
Cooper; London: Hamilton, 1959, 1979, 1990, 238 pp. One of the best military
accounts of the campaign; noted that Mountbatten and Montgomery opposed the
operation, the latter especially doubtful about collusion with Israel; Britain and
France suffered 155 casualties, 26 dead; considered a diplomatic and imperial
debacle; changed the course of British history.

136   Galatin, I.J. "The Resolution of Polaris." NIPROC, 111 (April 1985):
80-88. An authoritative summary of the background of Anglo-American defense
and nuclear weapons policies and agreements; in 1961 the U.S. committed five
Polaris submarines to NATO; meantime the British independent nuclear deterrent
vehicles, the Blue Steel, Blue Streak, and Skybolt were abandoned; the Naussau
Agreement of 1962 provided Polaris missiles for five (later four) British SSBNs.

137 "Gandhi." Movie. Dir: Richard Attenborough; starring Ben Kingsley; won 8 Academy Awards; dedicated to Nehru and Mountbatten; negative view of Jinnah.

138 Gardiner, Juliet. "Infamous Rehearsals." The Guardian (20 May 1994), pp. 4-5. The special 50th anniversary D-Day issue of this major British The Guardian; the Gardiner piece brought up again the Dieppe imbroglio, "the sea equivalent of the Charge of the Light Brigade."

139 Garlock, Peter David. "The U.S. and the Indian Crisis, 1941-1943: The Limits of Anti-colonialism." Ph.D. diss. Yale, 1972, 516 pp. Extensive background information of Anglo-American relations concerning India; FDR sent two missions demonstrating sympathy for the Indian nationalists: Louis Johnson and William Phillips; both recommended support for the nationalists; FDR ignored them and supported British suppression and jailing of nationalist leaders; maintenance of the Anglo-American alliance was more important.

140 Garrett, Richard. Motoring and the Mighty. London: Paul, 1971, 231 pp. A series of stories about fabulous cars and famous drivers; in the 1920s the Mountbattens owned Rolls-Royces and both drove at high speeds around the Broadlands estate.

141 -------. The Raiders: Elite Strike Forces which Altered the Coruse of War and History. NY: Van Nostrand, 1980, 224 pp. An illustrated history of raiding forces, including British Commandos, founded in 1940; participation; Mountbatten at COHQ oversaw raids on the Norwegian coast, Bruneval, St. Nazaire, and Dieppe.

142 Gilbert, Martin and Churchill, Randolph, eds. Winston S. Churchill. 8 vols. London: Heinemann; Boston: Houghton, 1961-1989, 8856 pp. The official biography of Churchill (1874-1965), begun by the son, Randolph (d. 1968), and Gilbert took over upon his death; a massive project which is to include about 20 companion volumes, several still to be published; Timothy Ash, a reviewer, called it more than monumental, "a museum of historical scholarship"; "nothing new" is a recurring assessment by reviewers; Churchill was responsible for appointments of Mountbatten to COHQ and SAC SEAC.

143 Giuseppi, Montagu S. Guide to the Contents of the Public Record Office. 3 vols. London: HMSO, 1923, 1963, 1969, 860 pp. The location of all official papers of all of the departments of the government of Great Britain, e.g., official records of COHQ, SEAC, Admiralty, and Defence Ministry.

144   Glendevon, Baron John Hope. <u>Viceroy at Bay: Lord Linlithgow in India, 1936-1943</u>. London: Collins, 1971, 288 pp. A biography of the Marquess of Linlithgow, a predecessor of Wavell whom Mountbatten succeeded as Viceroy of India; by his son.

145   Gooch, John. "The Chiefs of Staff and the Higher Organization for Defence in Britain, 1904-1984." <u>NWCR</u>, 49 (January 1986): 53-65. A history and analysis of the office of chief of staff, initially applicable to the army but later for the navy and airforce; Mountbatten was First Sea Lord and Chief of the Defence Staff after World War II.

146   Gopal, Sarvepalli. <u>Jawaharlal Nehru: A Biography</u>.   3 vols. Cambridge: Harvard UP, 1956-1984, 1080 pp.; abridged, NY: Oxford UP, 1993, 512 pp. The standard biography of Nehru, the key figure in the transfer of power; close friend of the Mountbattens, perhaps the lover of Lady Mountbatten.

147   Gracey, Sir Douglas. Papers. Liddell Hart Centre, King's College, London. The papers of General Gracey, British army commander of the force which occupied Indochina immediately after the war, later facilitating the return of the French.

148   Grigg, John, ed. <u>Nehru Memorial Lectures, 1966-1991</u> London and New Delhi: Oxfod UP, 1992, 275 pp. A series of 15 lectures by distinguished presenters on Nehru and modern India sponsored by the Jawaharlal Nehru Memorial Trust set up in the United Kingdom by Mountbatten.

149   Gueritz, E.F. "Nelson's Blood: Attitudes and Actions of the Royal Navy, 1939-1945." <u>JCONTEMHIS</u>, 16 (July 1981): 487-99. On the traditions and image of the Royal Navy perpetuated during World War II; a review of events, e.g., battle of the River Plate and sinking the <u>BISMARCK</u>, and leaders, e.g., A.B. Cunningham; however, Mountbatten was seen as a "newcomer" and an "outsider," not one of the "band of brothers."

150   Halpern, Paul G., ed. <u>The Keyes Papers: Selections from the Private and Official Correspondence of Admiral of the Fleet Baron Keyes of Zeebrugge</u>. <u>Navy Records Society</u> series. 3 vols. London: NRS, 1972-1981, 1469 pp. Vols. 117, 122, 123; Keyes participated in the Gallipoli campaign and led the Zeebrugge raid during World War I; Churchill recalled him to head COHQ but soon replaced him with Mountbatten.

151   -------. The Naval History of World War I. Annapolis: NIP, 1994, 1995, 614 pp. The new standard naval history of the war; extensive coverage of all participants and areas; Halpern had previously fully covered the Mediterranean phase, now expanded just as thoroughly to cover all areas.

152   Hamid, S. Shahid. Disastrous Twilight: A Personal Record of the Partition of India. London: Cooper, 1986, 383 pp. Foreword by Philip Ziegler; by the secretary to the Commander-in-Chief of the Indian Army before the transfer, a Muslim from Pakistan; a personal memoir; saw Mountbatten as puppet of Congress Party; Nehru played to his vanity and ambition brilliantly.

153   Hamilton, Nigel. Monty. 3 vols. London: Hamilton; NY: McGraw, 1981-1986, 2807 pp., abridged, NY: Random House, 1994, 653 pp. The standard biography of Field Marshal Montgomery; much praise of Montgomery; first volume pertinent for planning of Dieppe; Montgomery participated but then opposed execution and criticized Mountbatten.

154   Hampshire, A. Cecil. The Royal Navy since 1945: Its Transition to the Nuclear Age. London: Kimber, 1975, 288 pp. Foreword by Sir Peter Hill-Norton; a summary of the three decades after the war; Mountbatten was First Sea Lord, 1955-1959; the transition and draw-down culminating in nuclear power and nuclear warheads on missiles.

155   -------. Royal Sailors. London: Kimber, 1971, 224 pp. British dukes and princes serving in the Royal Navy since the seventeenth century; included Prince Louis of Battenberg (46 years), Mountbatten, the Duke of Edinburgh, and Prince Charles.

156   Hankins, Cyril. A History of the Battenberg Family. 2 vols. Unpublished typescript, 400 pp. Re several close relatives of Mountbatten: his father, Prince Louis, later first Marquess of Milford Haven and Lord Leopold Mountbatten, also born at Windsor, changed names to Mountbatten in 1917, and died in 1922.

157   Harris, Kenneth. Attlee. London, 1982, 640 pp. Biography of the Prime Minister, 1945-1951; pertinent sections on the end of empire; Attlee admired the effort of Mountbatten to resolve the situation in Burma; it became a model; Mountbatten to India as Viceroy; background on the situation in India; Attlee underestimated Jinnah and the Muslims; Mountbatten arrived 20 March 1947 and set date for 15 August; forced Congress and Muslims to act.

158   -------. Conversations. London: Hodder, 1967, 296 pp. Published interviews with 19 leaders, many reprints for the BBC; Mountbatten (pp. 138-59) recalled war experiences: anticipated command of aircraft carrier and upset when order to COHQ; failure of Dieppe meant preparation of Mulberry harbor for Normandy invasion; praise for Churchill as inspiration, especially 1940-1941.

159   Harwood, David. Alert to Danger. Foreword by Earl Mountbatten. London: Bell, 1969, 155 pp. Stories of courageous persons, e.g., Royal Life Saving Society with Mountbatten as Grand President; explanation of types of rescues.

160   Hastings, Stephen L.E. The Murder of TSR-2. London: Macdonald, 1966, 206 pp. An exotic jet bomber capable of carrying nuclear weapons was being developed by the RAF; after his retirement, Mountbatten denounced the project and stressed superiority of naval vehicles, aircraft carriers and submarines; plane cancelled and Nassau-Polaris agreement announced.

161   Hatch, Alden. The Mountbattens: The Last Royal Success Story. London: Allen; NY: Random House, 1965, 1966, 480 pp. Three biographies, 3 generations of British naval figures: Prince Louis, Lord Louis Mountbatten, and Prince Philip.

162   Heald, Tim. The Duke: A Portrait of Prince Philip. Alt. title: Philip: A Portrait of the Duke of Edinburgh. London: Hodder; NY: Morrow, 1991, 285 pp.   A biography of the Consort and husband of Queen Elizabeth; Mountbatten was his mentor and sponsor.

163   Henry, Hugh G. Dieppe Through the Lens of the German War Photographer. St. Catherine, Ont: Vanwell, 1993, 1994,, 64 pp. Super-folio size with full page black and white photos; a photographic record, e.g., numerous derelict tanks abandoned on the beach; Dieppe saw the first use of tanks for amphibious landings and a new tank landing ship.

164   Henshaw, Peter J. "The British Chiefs of Staff Committee and the Preparation of the Dieppe Raid, March-August 1942: Did Mountbatten Really Evade the Committee's Authority." War in History, 1 (July 1994): 197-214. An elaboration on the Brian Villa thesis: Mountbatten executed the Dieppe raid without proper authority; Henshaw thesis: Churchill in his position of Prime Minister and Minister of Defence overrode lesser authorities.

165   -------.   "The Dieppe Raid: A Product of Misplaced Canadian Nationalism?: Notes and Comments." CANHISREV, 77 (June 1996): 250-66.

Reviewed the debate over Dieppe; contended the initiative and role of the Canadians and their commanders has been neglected, depicted as passive while Mountbatten proceeded illegally and Churchill pressured; in fact, it was the Canadians who insisted on independent control to the exclusion of British advisors such as Montgomery, and that the raid proceed because the season might pass with no action taken.

166   Higham, Charles and Moseley, Roy. <u>Elizabeth and Philip: The Untold Story of the Queen of England and Her Prince</u>. NY: Doubleday, 1991, 516 pp. By biographers of movie stars used to expose; included sensationalized account about Mountbatten and the intrigue over Royal titles; expose of Mountbatten with sexual eccentricities including sadomasochistic activities and affairs with young men (p. 396).

167   Higham, Robin, ed. <u>A Guide to the Sources of British Military History</u>. London: Routledge; Berkeley: U CA P, 1971, 651 pp. Sponsored by the Conference on British Studies; by the military bibliographer extraordinary; one of the earliest and standard guides to the literature; a series of historiographical essays by noted experts evaluating and integrating 1300 entries.

168   -------. "The History of the Second World War: British Official History Series." <u>LIBRARY QUARTERLY</u>, 34 (July 1964): 240-48. A description of the British official history of the war, projected 85 vols.; the approach was different from that of the U.S.

169   -------, ed. <u>Official Histories: Essays and Bibliographies from Around the World</u>. Manhattan: Kansas State UP, 1970, 656 pp. The history of official histories; a series of essays on how many countries have produced official histories of wars; a critique of official histories.

170   Hill, J.R., ed. <u>The Oxford Illustrated History of the Royal Navy</u>. NY and Oxford: Oxford UP, 1995, 496 pp. Folio size with many illustrations, some in color; consultant ed., Bryan Ranft; 14 essays by noted experts; pertinent chapters, 13 and 14, on the postwar navy (pp. 381-433); places the naval career of Mountbatten in context.

171   Hoare, Philip. <u>Noel Coward: A Biography</u>. London: Sinclair, 1995, 605 pp. A new biography of Coward by an intimate friend; access to Coward papers; Coward carefully created the image, the dressing gown and decadance; of noted importance was the movie, "In Which We Serve."

172   Hoey, Brian. Mountbatten: The Private Story. London: Sidgwick, 1994, 282 pp.   By a media correspondent who conducted radio and TV interviews with Mountbatten, his daughters, Prince Philip, and others; since he claimed he verified every fact by research in the Mountbatten archive, so no need for footnotes; claimed this was the first intimate portrait of Mountbatten; he was "the vainest man alive" and "the consummate name-dropper" (pp. 1-5); much detail about the funeral, September 1979, fully arranged by Mountbatten since the late 1960s; rumors about homosexuality were not true, but private secretary and friends were, e.g., Noel Coward; poorly organized and hard to follow.

173   Holman, Dennis. Lady Louis: Life of the Countess Mountbatten of Burma. London: Hamlyn, 1952, 191 pp.   Frontispiece, a color portrait in uniform; other color photos; a popular format for a biographical study.

174   Horan, David W. Raiders or Elite Infantry?: The Changing Role of the U.S. Army Rangers from Dieppe to Grenada. Contributions in Military Studies. Westport, CT: Greenwood, 1992, 294 pp.   The development of specialized infantry units for the U.S. Army; earliest experience was at Dieppe where 50 Rangers participated (7 died or missing); extensive and impressive bibliography.

175   Horan, H.E. "OPERATION CHARIOT: The Raid on St. Nazaire, 17-28 March 1942." JRUSI, 106 (November 1961): 561-66. Because the German battleship TIRPITZ could use the large drydock at St. Nazaire, it was picked as the target for a raid; Mountbatten was in charge; an old "f-piper" American destroyer was used to crash the drydock gate; successful operation putting the drydock and port out of action for the duration.

176   Hough, Richard A. Bless Our Ship: Mountbatten and the KELLY. London: Hodder, 1991, 218 pp. By a prolific naval historian and commentator on the Mountbatten family; HMS KELLY was sunk in operations off Crete, 130 of her crew killed; Mountbatten was rescued out of the water and taken to Egypt; Mountbatten was not a great seaman or a fighting leader; HMS KELLY experienced several avoidable accidents.

177   -------. Born Royal: The Lives and Loves of the Young Windsors. NY: Bantam, 1988, 329 pp. While writing about the Mountbattens, this aside on the 6 children of George V, cousins of Mountbatten.

178   -------. Edwina: Countess Mountbatten of Burma. London: Weidenfeld; New York: Morrow, 1983, 1984, 253 pp.   Began with a genealogical table, Edwina Cynthia Annette Ashley, the granddaughter of Sir Ernest Cassel; ancestors were Shaftesbury and Palmerston; she was from high society and one of the wealthiest women of Britain; in the 1940s she expanded her charitable work, e.g., the Save the Children Fund and the St. John's Ambulance Brigade; she died in 1960 while on an inspection tour for the latter.

179   -------. Louis and Victoria: The Family History of the Mountbattens. Alt. title: The Mountbattens. London: Hutchinson; NY: Dutton, 1974, 1975, 1984, 441 pp. Prince Louis of Battenberg changed names in 1917, husband of the granddaughter of Queen Victoria; Lord Beresford and others accused him of pro-German inclinations; the pressure forced him to resign as First Sea Lord in 1914; Mountbatten commissioned this biography of his parents.

180   -------. Mountbatten: Hero of Our Time. London and New York: Random House, 1980, 1981, 317 pp. Dedicated "to his memory"; one of the important biographies by the chronicler of the family; an informal survey of his life before the Broadlands papers were available; recounted early life; to Osborne Naval College, Dartmouth, and thence to HMS LION, later to Cambridge University; salient dates of naval and political career; retired from Royal Navy in 1965, continuing charity work (involved in over 200 organizations); assassinated in a boat at Classiebawn Castle, County Sligo, Republic of Ireland, near Donegal Bay where three galleons of the Spanish Armada had crashed ashore in 1588 (Hough said 1585).

181   -------. Other Days Around Me: A Memoir. London: Hodder, 1992, 232 pp. Hough, who wrote a total of 95 books including naval histories, spent a significant part of his career chronicling the Mountbatten family; recollections of the association with Mountbatten (pp. 170-225); access to Broadlands papers and long interviews and travels with Mountbatten; Hough was on a cruise in HMS BRITANNIA in the Pacific with Prince Philip and Mountbatten; Mountbatten took Hough on a tour of his dynastic home, Schloss Heiligenberg on the Rhine; details on relations with Barbara Cartland, a prolific novelist and close friend of Edwina, the Contesss Mountbatten, later an intimate, "but not bed . . . ," friend and collaborator of Mountbatten; Hough did not believe Mountbatten was homosexual; learned of Edwina's affairs from her sister and from Barbara Cartland; Hough admitted the family opposed publication of this biography, but "it's what Mountbatten would have wanted"; noted that it went straight to the top of the bestseller list, half-a-million copies in hardback with more in the U.S. and foreign language editions.

182   Howard, Sir Michael. The Central Organisation of Defence. London: RUSI, 1970, 63 pp. By the distinguished military analyst and historian; the background and process of the reform culminating in the unified Ministry of Defence with Mountbatten as the first Chief of Defence Staff, the highest professional military office; he served from 1959-1965; Peter Thorneycroft was Minister of Defence; the initiative was from Mountbatten.

183   Howarth, Stephen, ed. <u>Men of War: Great Naval Leaders of World War II</u>. London: Weidenfeld; NY: St. Martin, 1992, 1993, 624 pp. Foreword by Lord Lewin; a series of biographical essays; Mountbatten not included; included were King, Nimitz, Yamamoto, Donitz, Cunningham, Ramsay, Somerville, Fraser, Godfrey, and Pound.

184   Htin Aung, U. <u>The Stricken Peacock: Anglo-Burmese Relations, 1752-1948</u>. Hague: Nijhoff, 1965, 142 pp. By a professor at the Universityl of Rangoon; a history of Anglo-Burmese relations from the perspective of Burman nationalism; anti-British with the Burmese as perpetually right.

185   Hudson, Henry V. <u>The Great Divide: Britain-India-Pakistan</u>. London: Hutchinson; NY: Atheneum; NY: Oxford UP, 1969, 1971, 1985, 602 pp. A history of the transfer of power; Mountbatten was Viceroy only 20 weeks: 20 weeks after his arrival he announced the transfer would occur in 10 weeks; concluded Mountbatten was scrupulously fair and professionalism of the Indian army prevented collapse.

186   Hughes, Edward Arthur. <u>The Royal Naval College, Dartmouth</u>. London: Winchester, 1950, 175 pp. A history of RNC Dartmouth which originated from the training ship <u>ILLUSTRIOUS</u> in the 1850s; training began for 23 cadets in 1857; land-based training began about 1900; RNC Osborne was founded in 1903, providing for the first two years of naval officer training, Dartmouth to provide the final two years; Mountbatten attended Osborne and Dartmouth.

187   Hughes-Hallett, J. "The Mounting of Raids." <u>JRUSI</u>, 95 (February 1950): 580-88. A memoir by the Canadian admiral responsible for planning raids for COHQ, first under Keyes and later under Mountbatten; apologetics, noted that as plans for Dieppe became more complicated due to weather and withdrawals of support, e.g., shore bombardment and pre-attack bombing; but pressure to do something before it was too late mounted.

188   Humphrey-Smith, Cecil, <u>et al</u>., eds. The Cambridge Armorial: Compiled by the Members of the Cambridge University Heraldic and Genealogical Society. Foreword by Earl Mountbatten. London: Orbis, 1985, 141 pp. An account of coats-of-arms and the heraldic tradition at Cambridge.

189   Hunter, Charles N. GALAHAD. San Antonio: Naylor, 1963, 248 pp. By a colonel, U.S. Army, successor to Frank Merrill, commander of of 5307th Composite Unit, better known as Merrill's Marauders; OPERATION GALAHAD, 1943-1944, long-range-penetration group (LRPG) operations in the Burma campaign identical to those of Orde Wingate; a critique of C-B-I command structures, especially opposition to Stilwell; the operations were under the overall command of Mountbatten who inspected the force as did Noel Coward.

190   Hunter, T. Murray. Canada at Dieppe. Canadian War Memorial History Publication. Toronto: Balmuir, 1982, 70 pp. Foreword by C.P. Stacey, the official historian of Canadian operations in World War II; folio size with 8 color paintings by Canadian war artists; a 40th anniversary commemoration; noted OPERATION RUTTER superseded by OPERATION JUBILEE was costly in Canadian casualties but not fruitless and wasteful; valuable experience was gained; an analytical and historical approach without the rancor which often characterized Canadian assessments.

191   Inder Singh, Anita. The Origins of the Partition of India, 1936-1947. South Asian Studies series. NY: Oxford UP, 1987, 285 pp. From an Oxford dissertation; re the background and process of the transfer of power which was followed by; horrific communal carnage; thesis: partition was not necessary, the British continued their philosophy of divide and rule, in this case, divide and quit; Jinnah gained undeserved influence; he did not represent true Muslim unity; actually the Muslims were seriously divided themselves.

192   "In Which We Serve." Movie. United Artists, 1942, 115 min. The controversial, widely acclaimed, and very successful war film directed, produced, written by and starring Noel Coward, along with David Lean and John Mills; Mountbatten and the loss of HMS KELLY were the inspiration of what became a patriotic and morale-boosting film in Great Britain; Mountbatten intervened when there was opposition from the Admiralty and facilitated the completion; Coward was awarded a special Oscar.

193   Jackson, Sir William and Bramall, Lord Dwin. The Chiefs: The Story of the United Kingdom Chiefs of Staff. London: Brassey; NY: Macmillan, 1992, 1993, 530 pp. The first comprehensive account to the top military leaders of Great Britain, the "Top Brass"; Bramall himself was Chief of Defence Staff, 1982-1985; the origins of the highest military-naval professional position were from failures during the Boer War and the formation of the Committee of Imperial Defence (CID); the structure became a model for the U.S. and other national defense organizations; Chapter 10, "The Mountbatten Era" (pp. 309-50);

included Kitchener, Jellicoe, Alanbrooke, Montgomery, and Mountbatten, his "era" being 1957-1964.

194   Jalal, Ayesha. The Sole Spokesman: Jinnah, the Muslim League and the Demand for Pakistan. Cambridge South Asian Studies. NY: Cambridge UP, 1985, 323 pp. A precise narrative of events of 1947 in India; claimed Mohammad Ali Jinnah (1876-1948) was against partition, thus a revisionist view; Jinnah sought parity for Muslims, not separation; the British decision to set a date and withdraw forced subsequent events; the result was two Dominions, the largest transfer of populations in recorded history; claimed Mountbatten was repeatedly partial to Nehru and the Congress Party.

195   Johnson, Franklyn A. Defence by Committee: The British Committee of Imperial Defence, 1885-1959. London: Oxford UP, 1960, 426 pp. Foreword by Lord Ismay. A scholarly history and analysis of the early defence structure for Great Britain which became a model for others; useful and informative bibliography; began with the creation of the Committee of Imperial Defence (CID) by Prime Minister Arthur Balfour in 1902, a response to spectacular failures of British forces in the Boer War.

196   -------. Defence by Ministry: The British Ministry of Defence, 1944-1974. Foreword by Earl Mountbatten. NY: Holmes, 1980, 253 pp. A sequel to the previous entry; covered from the administrations of Churchill to Wilson; Attlee had encouraged unification since the 1920s, Mountbatten was the key initiator and implementor of unification of the forces, serving as the first Chief of Defence Staff for 6 years; Mountbatten recalled early joint operations at COHQ; Duncan Sandys implemented the creation of the Ministry.

197   -------. "Defence by Ministry: The Mountbatten Legacy." Unpublished paper, University Seminars on the Armed Forces and Society, Chicago, 1983. A scholarly paper presented to a conference.

198   -------. "Restructuring the Armed Forces: Lord Louis Mountbatten and the British Approach to the Problem." CANDEFQTR, 15 (March 1986): 34-38. An overview of the reorganization of Canadian defense forces, using as the model the processes initiated by Mountbatten, later Chief of the Defence Staff of Great Britain; he was the principal architect of the most far-reaching military reorganization in modern British history; his goal was to reduce duplication and inefficiency; it was successfully tested in the Falklands/Malvinas campaign of 1982.

199   Johnson, Roy Frank. The ROYAL GEORGE. Foreword by Earl Mountbatten. London: Knight, 1971, 201 pp. About the catastrophic loss of this warship, a flagship sunk at anchor at Spithead with loss of 900 lives; a revisionist thesis on how and why it sank.

200   Jordan, Gerald, ed. Naval Warfare in the Twentieth Century, 1900-1945: Essays in Honour of Arthur Marder. Foreword by Earl Mountbatten. London: Croom Helm; NY: Russak, 1977, 243 pp. A series of essays by experts to honor the noted British naval historian, Arthur Marder; essayists included Paul Kennedy, Robin Higham, W.A.B. Douglas, and Barry Hunt and Donald Schurman, the latter on Dieppe (pp. 186-209); the essay placed Dieppe in the context of the development of British amphibious warfare doctrine and practice; only Winston Churchill perceived the potential of these offensive-type operations; slow development and limited number of landing craft precluded anything ambitious; Mountbatten insisted some operation must take place during the summer of 1942; Dieppe was the last operation of the "old raids policy."

201   Judd, Denis. Prince Philip, Duke of Edinburgh: A Biography. New York: Atheneum, 1980, 1981, 272 pp. The blurb described Philip as controversial, unconventional, and misunderstood; chapter 12, "The Mountbatten Connection" (pp. 189-202); Mountbatten was a father-figure to Philip, eventually he takes the Mountbatten name; in 1960 the royal family name became "Mountbatten-Windsor"; Beaverbrook press was persistently anti-Mountbatten; Mountbatten continued the very special relationship with Prince Charles.

202   Kadel, Robert J., ed. "Where I Came In . . . ." in China, Burma, India. Paducah, KY: Turner, 1986, 384 pp. Folio size with colored illustrations; dedication with photo: "SAC Lord Lewis [sic] Mountbatten" but "Louis" correctly spelled in text; a panegyric to prominent personalities of C-B-I: Mountbatten, Slim, Chiang, Wingate, Stilwell, Chennault, and Philip Cochran, said to be the model of a character in the comic strip "Terry and the Pirates"; C-B-I called "that low priority, forgotten hell hole; Hump fliers followed the 'Aluminum Trail'," the wreckage of C-46 cargo planes; a poetic tribute to Mountbatten by Frank Owen: "his charm, his energy, his sense of urgency. . . a man of purpose . . . the youngest Royal Navy captain of his time, younger than Nelson, the youngest admiral of the Royal Navy of all time" (p. 150).

203   Kemp, Peter Kemp, ed. The Oxford Companion to Ships and the Sea. NY and London: Oxford, 1976, 1988, 978 pp. A monumental reference guide to maritime history edited by the much revered naval historian, 3700 entries on battles, ports, and biographical sketches, e.g., Marquess of Milford Haven, father of Mountbatten and Mountbatten (pp. 562-64): "sometimes mistaken as playboy" and credited with reorganization of the 3 services into the Ministry of Defence.

204   Kent, Barrie. Signal!: A History of Signalling in the Royal Navy. Hampshire: Hyden, 1993, 384 pp. Foreword by Sir Edward Ashmore; a history of communication systems used in the Royal Navy, e.g., from the shutter system to modern satellites; Mountbatten (pp. 74-78) contributed significantly as a specialist in signals and wireless during the 1920s and 1930s.

205   Kerr, Mark Edward Fredric. Prince Louis of Battenberg, Admiral of the Fleet. London: Longman, 1934, 317 pp. The father of Mountbatten, after 1917, Marquess of Milford Haven (1854-1921); career in the Royal Navy up to First Sea Lord, resigning in 1914 due to anti-German pressure; included genealogical tables.

206   Keyes, Lord Roger. Amphibious Warfare and Combined Operations. NY: Macmillan, 1943, 101 pp. The Lee Knowles Lectures by the recent COHQ director; emphasis on interservice cooperation; 5 case studies: Quebec, Boxer Rebellion, Dardanelles, Zeebrugge, and Commandos in the early 1940s, including Dieppe.

207   -------. The Naval Memoirs of Admiral of the Fleet Sir Roger Keyes. 2 vols. London: Thornton, 1934-1935, 816 pp. Informative and interesting about his career and the development of amphibious and combined operations, but also opinionated and belligerent.

208   King, Norman, et al. All the Queen's Men: The Profession of Arms: Navy, Army and Air Force. Foreword by Earl Mountbatten. Reading: Explorers, 1967, 148 pp. At the time of the integration of the 3 services in Great Britain, essays on each of the armed forces, sailor, soldier, airman.

209   Kirby, S. Woodburn. Singapore: The Chain of Disaster. Foreword by Earl Mountbatten. London: Cassell; NY: Macmillan, 1971, 285 pp. By the official British historian of the Asian/Pacific War; one of the noted accounts of the spectacular and humiliating defeat of the British force by the Japanese; the British base which was constructed during the 1920s was to be the impregnable bastion of the British empire in the East; the Japanese conquered all of Malaya with a force inferior in numbers.

210   Kirby, S. Woodburn, et al. The War against Japan. Official History of the Second World War series. 5 vols. London: HMSO, 1957-1969, 2735 pp. The official British history of the Asian/Pacific War; the British armed forces were the most active in the China-Burma-India theater, the area of SEAC, under the command Mountbatten.

211   Kiriakopoulos, G.C. Ten Days to Destiny: The Battle for Crete, 1941. NY and London: Watts, 1985, 413 pp. May 1941, German air and airborne forces fought fiercely and captured the island of Crete from British land and naval forces; a major victory for German paratroopers but it never operated again; HMS KELLY was sunk during this campaign.

212   Kirkpatrick, Lyman B., Jr. Captains without Eyes: Intelligence Failures in World War II. NY: Macmillan, 1969, 317 pp. An assessment of the role of intelligence in war; several case studies of intelligence failures, including Dieppe and Pearl Harbor.

213   Krishan, Y. "Mountbatten and the Partition of India." History, 68 (February 1983): 22-37. An indictment of the British government and its handling of the transfer of power, especially the failure to maintain law and order; there was no preparation for the mass migrations which occurred; the political leaders reached agreement to divide but failed to save the country from massacres; the transfer was too hurried and premature; Mountbatten accelerated the process on his own initiative partly because of the upcoming royal wedding in November 1947.

214   Kyi, Aung San Suu. Aung San. Leaders of Asia series. St. Lucia: U Queensland P, 1984, 42 pp. By the Nobel Peace Prize winner; a biography of her father, Aung San (1915-1947), the Burmese leader, founder of the Burma Independent Army which collaborated with the Japanese during the occupation; then formed the Anti-Fascist People's Freedom League; Mountbatten was sympathetic of the nationalists; most likely Aung San would have been leader of Burma but assassinated, July 1947.

215   Kyle, Keith. Suez. London: Weidenfeld; NY: St. Martin, 1991, 673 pp. By a journalist who first produced a TV documentary and then a scholarly research project including British, American, French, and Israeli sources; a standard, full-length narrative of the crisis and campaing of 1956; tripartite collusion was unquestioned; Anglocentric view focusing on Eden; the debacle was partly due to the poor health of Eden.

216   Ladd, James D. Commandos and Rangers of World War II. Foreword by Earl Mountbatten. NY: St. Martin, 1978, 288 pp. A comprehensive survey of several special force units; in his foreword Mountbatten recalled 10 Commando when he was at COHQ, General George Marshall visited, April

1942, the basis for initiation of the Rangers; 2 Commando was at St. Nazaire, 4 Commando at Dieppe; other special forces in Burma and the Philippines.

217   -------. The Royal Marines, 1919-1980: An Authorized History. London: Jane, 1980, 482 pp. Foreword by HRH Prince Philip, protege of Mountbatten; an official history of the Royal Marines, the "Sea Soldiers"; included the evolution of amphibious and commando services.

218   Lahr, John. "Whiz Kid of the West End: Noel Coward." New Yorker (September 4, 1995): 96-98. A study of Noel Coward and his accomplishments, e.g., 60 stage plays, 12 films, 300 songs, and a 3-vol. autobiography; "In Which We Served" brought Coward a special Oscar.

219   Lambton, Antony. The Mountbattens: The Battenbergs and Young Mountbatten. London: Constable, 1989, 256 pp. A collective biography of the family, Prince Louis and Princess Alexandra and Lord Louis Mountbatten; undistinguished.

220   Lane, Peter. Prince Philip. London: Hale, 1980, 352 pp. A biography of Prince Philip, his parents, Prince Andrew and Princess Alice Battenberg of Greece; they escaped from Greece in 1922 and had no permanent home; Chapter 10 on "Lord Louis" (pp. 75-90) and extensive discussion on the "name" issue.

221   Langdon, Jeremy. "Too Old or Too Bold?: The Removal of Sir Roger Keyes as Churchill's First Director of Combined Operations." IMPWARMUSREV, 8 (n.d.): 72-84. Keyes was made Director, COHQ in July 1940 and removed by Churchill on 19 October 1941; he had participated in the Dardanelles and led the Zeebrugge campaigns; he resented the removal; he remained a backbencher, MP for Portsmouth North until going to the House of Lords in 1943.

222   "The Last Viceroy." TV Documentary. PBS, 1968. Re Mountbatten as Viceroy of India; generally historically correct.

223   Law, Derek G. The Royal Navy in World War II: An Annotated Bibliography. London: Greenhill; Novato, CA: Presidio, 1988, 305 pp. A useful guide to the literature divided by topics containing 1883 briefly annotated entries published in English up to 1988.

224   Leasor, James. Green Beach. NY: Morrow, 1975, 292 pp. A fictional account of the Dieppe operation; anecdotal with little background; focused on an intelligence objective: to seize parts of the German radar sets to ascertain technological capabilities.

225   -------. Boarding Party. Foreword by Earl Mountbatten. Boston: Houghton; Annapolis: NIP, 1979, 1995, 224 pp. Re naval operations in the Indian Ocean during the war; 14 untitled chapters; account of secret missions, e.g., a raid on a transmitter in India communicating with German U-boats operating in the Indian Ocean; the result was virtually eliminating sinkings of Allied shipping.

226   Lee, Loyd E., ed. World War II in Europe, Africa, and the Americas, with General Sources: A Handbook of Literature and Research. 2 vols. Westport: Greenwood, 1997, 535 pp. An extensive bibliographical and research guide to sources about World War II presented in a series of essays by expert scholars; A second volume, World War II in Asia and the Pacific and the War's Aftermath: A Handbook of Literature and Research is forthcoming in 1998.

227   Leigh, Vida. Mary Bright of Fiddlers Green. Foreword by Earl Mountbatten. Cheadle, Cheshire: Galt, n.d., 91 pp. The foreword was handwritten in 1966; recollections of Leigh, a resident of Ireland near Calssiebawn Castle, County Sligo, near the Mountbatten estate.

228   Lepotier, Adolphe Auguste Marie. Raiders from the Sea. London: Kimber, 1954, 200 pp. A French account in English of the St. Nazaire and Dieppe raids.

229   Lesley, Cole. The Life of Noel Coward. (Published in U.S. under: Remembered Laughter by Knopf.) NY: Knopf, 1976, 1977, 521 pp. A biography of Coward; many citations about Mountbatten.

230   Lesley, Cole, et al. Noel Coward and His Friends. NY: Morrow, 1979, 216 pp. Mountbatten is included in the various accounts.

231   Lewin, Ronald. The Chief: Field Marshal Lord Wavell: Commander-in-Chief and Viceroy, 1939-1947. NY: Farrar, 1980, 282 pp. By the distinguished biographer; a biography of Wavell, army commander and Viceroy of India.

232   -------. Churchill as War Lord. NY: Stein, 1973, 291 pp. Depicted Churchill as constantly intervening in military and naval affairs, a man of excess: emotion, energy, egocentricity, and courage.

233 -------. Slim, the Standard Bearer: A Biography of Field Marshal the Viscount Slim. Hamden: Shoe String, 1976, 1990, 365 pp. An award-winning biography; full cooperation by the family and highly authentic; included the Burma campaign, retreat and advance; later Governor-General of Australia; many references to Mountbatten.

234 Lewin, Sir Terrence. The Mountbatten Memorial Lecture, 1980, given at the Royal United Services Institution, 7 July 1980, by Air Marshal Sir Terrence Lewin in the presence of the two daughters of Mountbatten; a review of the career and accomplishments of Mountbatten.

235 Lider, Julian. British Military Thought after World War II. Aldershot: Gower, 1984, 1985, 633 pp. An important appraisal sponsored by the Swedish Institute of International Affairs; reviewed contributions of military theorists, e.g., Slessor, Liddell Hart, Fuller, Montgomery, Howard, and King-Hall, government White Papers, think tanks, and periodicals; the pertinent phases were atomic deterrence, thermonuclear look, and independent nuclear forces; Mountbatten played an important role but was not listed among the theorists.

236 Lieven, D.C.B. The Aristocracy of Europe, 1815-1914. NY: Columbia UP; London: Macmillan, 1992, 332 pp. An overview of the aristocracy in Europe in the nineteenth century, their sources of wealth, life, manners, and morals; a section on the noble as warrior.

237 "The Life and Times of Lord Mountbatten." 13 parts. TV Documentary, 1966-1967, 388 minutes. The expert advisers were John Terraine and Peter Morley, Mountbatten himself doing the narrative; assistance from the Imperial War Museum; available through Fusion Video, Tinley Park, IL.

238 Liversidge, Douglas. The Mountbattens: From Battenberg to Windsor. London: Barker, 173 pp. A superficial collective biography by a journalist; a personal note by Mountbatten in his library copy: "The author never made contact with any of the family."

239 Lockhart, Sir Robert Bruce. The Marines Were There: The Story of the Royal Marines in the Second World War. London: Putnam, 1950, 229 pp. A regimental history, anecdotal; the Royal Marines participated in small wars in the nineteenth century, were at Gallipoli, Dieppe, Burma, and aboard RN ships in the Asian/Pacific War.

240   Lonn, George. British Portraits: Notable Personalities in Charcoal Sketches. Toronto: Pitt, 1984, 91 pp. On the front cover: a painting of Mountbatten; other charcoal drawings of Prince Philip and Viscount Slim.

241   Lorelli, John A. To Foreign Shores: U.S. Amphibious Operations in World War II. Annapolis: NIP, 1995, 416 pp. Foreword by Rolf Illsley; described the series of seaborne assaults, planning, tactics, landing craft, command, and first hand accounts; early initiatives were from the U.S. Marines; included Dieppe where there were problems but much was learned.

242   Lucas, W. Scott. Britain and Suez: The Lion's Last Roar. Manchester: UP; NY: St. Martin, 1996, 151 pp. A narrative and analysis of this campaign which "marked the end of the British empire."

243   -------. Divided We Stand: Britain, the U.S. and the Suez Crisis. London: Hodder, 1991, 411 pp. A scholarly account of the campaign and the international and special relationship implications.

244   -------. "Divided We Stand: The Suez Crisis of 1956 and the Anglo-American Alliance." Ph.D. diss, London, 1991. A dissertation, the basis of the previous entry.

245   MacBeth, George. The Katana: A Novel Based on the Wartime Diaries of John Beeby. NY: Simon, 1981, 239 pp. A first hand narrative format with a compelling plot; opened with an account of the assassination of Mountbatten in 1979; recalled service under Mountbatten in the Far East for 3 years and an earlier assassination attempt in 1944: a Japanese plot to blow up Mountbatten at Kandy; surprisingly, the narrator was a double agent who planned the attempt but was prevented from doing so; an implication that the successful operation was fruition of the earlier attempt.

246   McDonald, Kendall, ed. The Second Underwater Book: For the British Sub-Aqua Club. Foreword by Earl Mountbatten. London: Pelham, 1970, 274 pp. The First Underwater Book was published in 1968 and was a great success; Mountbatten recalled much personal experience using Cousteau Aqualung; a series of essays concluding with addresses of 300 British Sub-Aqua Clubs; HMS PRINCE OF WALES and REPULSE, in water off the Indochinese coast 180 feet deep, were discovered and marked by members.

247   McGeoch, Sir Ian. "The Way Astern: Why Not HMS FISHER?" AQ&DJ, 123 (April 1993): 144-48. Admiral McGeoch was concerned about the future of the Royal Navy in the early 1990s; recalled that in the 1950s

Mountbatten, when First Sea Lord, had similar concerns and formed the "Way Ahead Committee"; reforms equivalent to those of "Jacky" Fisher in 1904 followed; why not create an innovative officer training center and call it HMS FISHER?

248   -------. The Princely Sailor: Mountbatten of Burma. Wash: Brassey, 1996, 200 pp. A new biography of Mountbatten by a retired admiral, former editor of Naval Review, a professional journal; concluded that the achievements of Mountbatten outweighed his faults, e.g., creation of the central organization for Defence and the independence of India and Pakistan; all the while, he had proceeded from cadet to Admiral of the Fleet.

249   McInnes, Colin J. "The British Decision to Replace Her Polaris Nuclear Deterrent." Ph.D. diss. Wales, Aberstwyth, 1985. A dissertation about the background and the decision to replace the Polaris ballistic missile deterrent system with the more advanced Trident system, already deployed by American submarines; Mountbatten was instrumental in the making of the Polaris system.

250   Macintyre, Donald G.F.W. Fighting Admiral: A Life of Admiral of the Fleet Sir James Somerville. London: Evans, 1961, 270 pp. A biography of this prominent and controversial admiral during World War II; earlier as commander of naval Force H, operating out of Gibraltar, Somerville was faulted for permitting a French force being tracked to "escape" into the Atlantic; later, Somerville was naval chief of staff under Mountbatten as SAC SEAC; after a conflict, Somerville was sent home.

251   Macksey, Kenneth and Woodhouse, William.   The Penguin Encyclopedia of Military Warfare: 1850 to the Present Day. NY: Viking, 1991, 383 pp. A comprehensive encyclopedia; on Mountbatten (pp. 223-24).

252   Maguire, Eric. Dieppe, August 9. London: Cape, 1963, 205 pp. A highly charged narrative about the Dieppe raid of 1942, called "the blackest day in Canadian military history" (p. 11); a series of unnumbered chapters, e.g., "Anticipation," "Frustration," "Annihilation," and "Revelation."

253   "A Man of This Century: The Life and Times of Lord Mountbatten." Documentary. Twentieth-Century Leaders series. London: START, n.d., 6 hours.   Mountbatten personally assisted in the making of this extensive documentary on his life and times; shown on PBS and other networks.

254   Manning, Thomas D. and Walker, C.F. British Warship Names. Foreword by Earl Mountbatten. London: Putnam, 1959, 498 pp. By two officers in the Royal Navy; a dictionary of ship names, each entry including when, what, and participating battles; a separate essay on the Ship Names Committee.

255 Mansergh, Nicholas, et al., eds. Transfer of Power, 1942-1947. 12 vols. London: HMSO, 1970-1983, 1200 pp. Publication of official documents relating to the transfer of power; released and published early as ordered by Prime Minister Wilson; original publication date was to be 1999; sections on the Cripps Mission, "Quit India," "Mountbatten as Viceroyalty," and disposition of the "Princes."

256 March, Edgar J. British Destroyers: A History of Development, 1892-1953. Foreword by Earl Mountbatten. London: Seeley; Annapolis: NIP, 1966, 539 pp. Begun by Oscar Parkes who died, replaced by March; a distinguished and comprehensive study of an important warship type in the Royal Navy; thoroughly researched and detailed; e.g., the role of destroyers in the battle of Jutland of 1916 and inclusion of plans; curiously, nothing on the 50 American destroyers, designated the TOWN class, in the Destroyers-for-Bases deal.

257 "MARCO." Pseud. for Earl Mountbatten. An Introduction to Polo. Preface by Earl Mountbatten. London: Country Life; NY: Scribner, 1931, 1937, 1950, 1960, 1965, 1976, 1986, 152 pp. Foreword by Lord Wodehouse, later Earl of Kimberley; at least 8 editions; the standard introductory guide to polo; first issued by the Royal Naval Polo Association; Mountbatten noted a French translation/edition.

258 -------. "The Spectator at Polo." Chakkar, 1 (1986): 46-50. A copy of this article was in the Mountbatten Exhibition at Broadlands; included a photo of trophies won by Mountbatten as a polo player.

259 Marder, Arthur J., et al. Old Friends, New Enemies: The Royal Navy and the Imperial Japanese Navy. 2 vols. London: Oxford UP, 1981-1990, 1183 pp. The distinguished but flawed British naval historian died in 1980 and the monograph was finished by two of his doctoral students; the standard history of British-Japanese naval relations before and during World War II; extensive coverage in the second volume of the Royal Navy during the latter years of the war; Admiral Somerville figures prominently and Somerville-Mountbatten relationships were reviewed, e.g., Somerville objected to what he perceived to be lengthly, frequent, useless called conferences with Mountbatten; Marder sympathetic to Somerville; claimed the appointment of Mountbatten was ill-received within the navy; relations soured and Mountbatten appealed to Churchill who recalled Somerville; Mountbatten also contributed to debate over participation of Royal Navy, operating with the U.S. Navy, in the final months of the war; much detail on the Japanese navy.

260   Marx, Roland. Mort d'un amiral: l'IRA contre Mountbatten. Paris: Calmann-Levy, 1985, 231 pp. An account in French of the assassination of Mountbatten.

261   Mason, David. Raid on St. Nazaire. Ballatine History of World War II series. NY: Ballantine, 1970, 157 pp. A popular history with many illustrations of the St. Nazaire raid.

262   -------. Who's Who in World War II. Boston: Little Brown; London: Weidenfeld, 1978, 363 pp. A biographical dictionary of the leading figures of the war; Mountbatten (pp. 207-15) received comparatively large coverage plus two photos.

263   Masson, Madeline. Edwina: The Biography of the Countess Mountbatten of Burma. Foreword by Earl Mountbatten. London: Jarrolds; London: Hale, 1958, 1960, 1975, 272 pp. A portrait of Lady Mountbatten (d. 1960) by Salvador Dali was on the cover; a creditable biography; Mountbatten noted he received 6,000 telegrams and letters after her death; traced her descent to Kings Edward IV and Henry VII.

264   Matthews, Geoffrey F.   The Re-conquest of Burma, 1943-1945. Aldershot: Gate, 1966, 115 pp. Foreword by Piers Mackesy; a tactical and strategic overview of an important campaign for the British armed forces sponsored by the British Army Officer Staff College; decisive and the turning point was the battle of Kohima; Mountbatten figured prominently, as do Wingate and Stilwell.

265   Maund, L.E.H. Assault from the Sea: Combined Operations. London: Methuen, 1949, 327 pp. A memoir of Rear Admiral Maund, a staff officer, COHQ, describing operations and the lessons learned.

266   Maung, U. Maung. Burmese Nationalist Movements, 1940-1948. Honolulu: U Hawaii P, 1990, 402 pp. A limited and narrow history of the transfer of power in Burma; a description of the native Burmese leaders, their reaction and later cooperation during the Japanese occupation, then frustration; Mountbatten became increasingly sympathetic and was at odds with the British colonial administration, e.g., Dorman-Smith; praise for Aung San.

267 Menon, V.P. The Transfer of Power in India. London: Longman; Princeton: UP, 1957, 543 pp. A monograph, covering the transfer, 1939-1947, by a leading official in the process; Mountbatten praised his work; the role of Mountbatten was most important and all parties praised him.

268 -------. The Story of the Integration of the Indian States. Calcutta and London: Longman, 1956, 511 pp. The sequel to the previous entry; a monumental study.

269 Messenger, Charles. The Commandos, 1940-1946. London: Kimber, 1985, 447 pp. A survey of operations of these elite and special forces; originally formed after the Dunkirk retreat; accounts of the St. Nazaire and Dieppe raids.

270 Miall, Leonard, ed. Richard Dimbleby: Broadcaster. Foreword by Earl Mountbatten. London: BBC, 1966, 184 pp. A photo of Dimbleby interviewing Mountbatten; Dimbleday (d. 1965), the subject of 45 essays paising his contributions to the media.

271 Millar, George. The Bruneval Raid: Flashpoint of the Radar War. Foreword by Earl Mountbatten. London: Bodley; London: Pan, 1974, 1976, 224 pp. By a veteran COHQ officer who parachuted into France to capture an important radar installation; aided by the French Resistance; the raid occurred in February 1942; Mountbatten facilitated the research for the book.

272 Millington-Drake, Sir Eugene, comp. The Drama of the GRAF SPEE and the Battle of the River Plate: A Documentary Anthology, 1914-1964. Foreword by Earl Mountbatten. London: Davies, 1964, 1965, 536 pp. Preface by Sir Philip Vian; the British minister in Uruguay collected pertinent documents and reports and produced commentary, all describing the famous battle between British cruisers and the German pocket battleship, December 1939; seen as the last classic naval battle, no aircraft, no radar, etc; an authoritative account.

273 Mitchell L.M., et al, eds. A Summary Catalogue of the Papers of Earl Mountbatten of Burma. Occasional Papers # 9. Southampton: University Library, 1991, 315 pp. In 1988 the Trustees of the Broadlands Archives transferred its holdings to the Library of the University of Southampton, Southampton; about 250,000 papers, 50,000 photos, tapes, and film; a summary guide of the materials available to researchers; used extensively by Philip Ziegler for the official biography; examples of listed items: a newspaper produced at SEAC, Kandy, despatches, reports from the Viceroy, and the criticism of the Suez campaign of 1956.

274   Moir, Martin. <u>A General Guide to the India Office Records</u>. <u>British Library Publications</u>. London: BL, 1989. An excellent reference guide to official papers associated with India, including the East India Company and the transfer of power.

275   Moncrieff, Anthony, ed. <u>Suez: Ten Years After</u>. London: BBC; NY: Pantheon, 1966, 1967, 160 pp. Intro. by Peter Calvocoressi; an important ten year assessment of the campaign; a series of essays by participants and historians; the supporting book for an 8-part BBC programme, Third Programme.

276   Moon, Sir Penderel. <u>Divide and Quit</u>. Berkeley: U CA P, 1961, 1962, 302 pp. The end of the British Raj; recollections of tragic events associated with the transfer of power: massacres and migrations, thousands killed and millions displaced.

277   Moore, R.J.   <u>Churchill, Cripps, and India, 1939-1945</u>.   Oxford: Clarendon, 1979, 160 pp. Churchill consistently opposed independence for India; Moore contended he did all he could to sabotage the process; the Cripps Mission of 1942 ultimately failed.

278   -------. <u>Escape from Empire: The Attlee Government and the Indian Problem</u>. Oxford: Clarendon, 1983, 386 pp. A revisionist assessment of the transfer of power from the perspective of the Labor Government; Cripps was influential; Mountbatten was able to resolve the problem of the princely states with a brilliant slight of hand; summary of the price of partition.

279   -------.   "Mountbatten,   India,   and   the   Commonwealth." <u>JCOMMON&COMPARPOL</u> (1981): 5-43. A review of events associated with the transfer of power; precipitated communal outrage; contended partition could have been avoided; Mountbatten acted too rapidly.

280   Morgan, Janet P. <u>Edwina Mountbatten: A Life of Her Own</u>. London: HarperCollins; NY: Scribners, 1991, 504 pp. A biography written at the request of the two daughters of Lady Mountbatten (1901-1960); access to Broadlands papers; she was a multifacited person, very wealthy and a leader of high society; several affairs, e.g., with Bunny Phillips and Nehru, and several rows, e.g., talk of divorce in the 1950s.

281   Mosley, Leonard.   <u>The Last Days of the British Raj</u>.   London: Weidenfeld; NY: Harcourt, 1961, 1962, 263 pp. A survey of the last days of British rule by a journalist; noted that 15 million persons were forced to flee, 600,000 were killed; 1947 was "a bumper year for vultures"; blamed

Mountbatten for premature withdrawal and thus responsible for the massacres (pp. 243-47).

282 Mountbatten of Burma, Earl. Apocalypse Now?: Earl Mountbatten, Lord Noel-Baker, Lord Zukerman. Nottingham: Spokesman, 1980, 64 pp. A series of essays on the occasion of the U.N. Special Assembly on Disarmament; a speech by Mountbatten, "The Final Abyss?" (pp. 9-14), was made as part of the award of the Louise Weiss Foundation Prize to the Stockholm International Peace Research Institute, Strasbourg, 11 May 1979.

283 -------. "The Battle of Jutland: An Appreciation Given at the Annual Jutland Dinner in HMS WARRIOR on 25 May 1978." MM, 66 (May 1980): 99-111. A speech at this special occasion; recollections of his first assignment as a naval cadet, to HMS LION, flagship of Admiral David Beatty, arriving 7 weeks after the battle; the problems for the British at Jutland were defective shells, anti-flash protection, and insufficient armor protectiion.

284 -------. Electronics the Lifeline. London: Abell, 1978, 20 pp. A lecture by Mountbatten delivered to the National Electronics Council, 28 June 1978, at the Royal Institution.

285 -------. "Ma guerre contre les Aponais et la Mousson." Paris Match, 45/65 (August 21, 1965): 30-41. In French, an article about the experiences of Earl and Lady Mountbatten in the war.

286 -------. Mountbatten: Eighty Years in Pictures. A Studio Book. NY: Viking, 1979, 224 pp. Folio size; an illustrated bio-history of Mountbatten.

287 -------. Mountbatten and Independent India, 16 August 1947-18 June 1948. New Delhi: Vikas, 1984, 203 pp. An account of the time Mountbatten spent in India after independence; he was Governor-General.

288 -------. Mountbatten and Pakistan. Karachi: Quaid-i-Azam, 1982, 175 pp. A short overview of relations between Mountbatten and the new state of Pakistan.

289 -------. The Mountbatten Lineage: The Direct Descent of the Family of Mountbatten from the House of Brabant and the Rulers of Hesse. n.p., 1946, 1958, 458 pp. Noted as "Prepared for private circulation" by Mountbatten who was President, Society of Genealogists and Patron of the Cambridge University Heraldic and Genealogical Society; it took 11 years to compile; presented 44 generations (pp. 16-367); Brabant/Hessian/Mountbatten can be traced back to the

4th century A.D., including Clovis and Pippin; first prepared at the time Prince Philip changed his name to Mountbatten; the hope was that Queen Elizabeth would assume the family name of Mountbatten; thwarted first by Queen Mary and then by Elizabeth herself.

290   -------. "OPERATION JUBILEE: The Place of the Dieppe Raid in History." JRUSI, 119 (1974): 25-30. His personal recollections of the planning, rehearsals, and execution of the raid in August 1942; much was learned, e.g., that large ports could not be captured by frontal assault and the number of casualties at Normandy would be 12 times less.

291   -------. Personal Diary of Admiral the Lord Louis Mountbatten, 1943-1946. Ed. by Philip Ziegler. London: Collins, 1988, 357 pp. Publication of part of the diaries of Mountbatten as SAC SEAC, November 1943-June 1946; abridgment meant reduction by one-third

292   -------. Post Surrender Tasks: Section E of the Report to the Combined Chiefs of Staff. London: HMSO, 1969, 49 pp. A report compiled in 1947 from SAC SEAC to the Allied Combined Chiefs of Staff on activities and operations after the surrender of Japan; for Mountbatten the worst case was Indonesia; he was critical of the pigheadedness of the Dutch officials

293   -------. Report to the Combined Chiefs of Staff by the Supreme Allied Commander, South-East Asia, 1943-1945. London: HMSO; NY: Philosophical, 1951, 280 pp. A comprehensive and elaborate report to his superiors.

294   -------. Report of the Inquiry into Prison Escapes and Security. London: HMSO, 1966, 99 pp. A special investigation conducted by Mountbatten; the report.

295   -------. "The Strategy of the South-East Asia Campaign." JRUSI, 91 (November 1946): 469-84. An address to RUSI delivered 9 October 1946; an assessment of the war in Southeast Asia; noted the confused command structure; praise for the unprecedented air supply operations.

296   -------. Time Only to Look Forward: Speeches of Rear Admiral the Earl Mountbatten of Burma. London: Kaye, 1949, 283 pp. A series of speeches in chronological order, e.g., as Viceroy, as Governor-General, and upon his return to London to the East Indian Association, 19 June 1948.

297   Mountbatten, Edwina Cynthia Annette, Countess Mountbatten of Burma. Entry in The Dictionary of National Biography, 1951-1960. Oxford: UP, 1971,

pp. 751-53. The entry in DNB, by Alan Campbell-Jones; b. 28 November 1901, d. 21 February 1960; daughter of W.W. Ashley, Baron Mount Temple of Broadlands, Romsey and Classiebawn Castle, Co Sligo and granddaughter of Sir Ernest Cassel; godfather was King Edward VIII; married to Mountbatten in 1922; 1939, began career in St. John Ambulance Brigade, on missions throughout the world.

298 -------. Entry in Who Was Who, 1951-1960. NY: St. Martin, 1961, p. 795. A typical Who's Who entry presenting biographical background such as education, honors and titles, and association with organizations, e.g., educated at The Links, Eastbourne and Alde House, Aldeburgh and president, Save the Children Fund and associated with the Girl Guides; most prominent of her service was her work in St. John Ambulance Brigade Overseas.

299 Mountbatten, Louis Alexander, Prince of Battenberg. The Royal Navy, 1815-1914. Cambridge: UP, 1918, 48 pp. The Rede Lecture, 1918; by the father of Mountbatten, written at the end of World War I; a pamphlet, the history of the Royal Navy during the previous century.

300 Mountbatten, Louis Francis Albert Victor Nicholas, first Earl Mountbatten of Burma. Entry in The Dictionary of National Biography, 1971-1980. Oxford: UP, 1986, pp. 605-16. The entry in DNB, by Philip Ziegler, the official biographer; b. 25 June 1900, d. 27 August 1979; son of Prince Louis Alexander of Battenberg, later Louis Mountbatten, Marquess of Milford Haven; closely connected to the royal family, nephew of the last Tsar of Russia; "Dickie," after 1917, Lord Louis Mountbatten; to the Royal Navy in 1913; married to Edwina in 1922; service in the navy; director, COHQ, planned raid on Dieppe, August 1942; SAC SEAC, August 1943, taking over major problems and a complex command structure; HQ in Kandy, Ceylon; took foral surrender of the Japanese, Singapore, 12 September 1945; December 1946-August 1947, the last Viceroy of India; to June 1948, Governor-General of India; returned to Royal Navy becoming First Sea Lord, October 1954, and later, July 1959, Chief of Defence Staff, retiring in June 1965; TV series, 1966-1967; assassinated by the Irish Republican Army in 1979; funeral at Westminister Abbey; daughter Patricia succeeded as Countess Mountbatten of Burma.

301 -------. Entry in Who's Who, 1978-1979: Annual Biographical Dictionary. NY: St. Martin, 1978, pp. 1757-58. A typical entry in this well known biographical dictionary; most of the information in the next annotated entry was included.

302   -------. Entry in Who Was Who, Vol. VII, 1971-1980. Companion to
Who's Who. NY: St. Martin, 1981, p. 565. One of the longer entries in Who
Was Who, biographical listings of important persons who died in the decade; a
long list of the honors and awards received by Mountbatten and the orgainzations
with which he was associated; the honors are listed in the narrative section above
under Assessments; organizations included King George's Fund for Sailors, the
Society of Genealogists, the Britain-Burma Society, the Sea Scouts, the Royal
Swedish Naval Society, and founder of the National Electronics Research
Council.

303   Mountbatten obituary. "Admiral of the Fleet Earl Mountbatten." MM,
65 (November 1979): 285-88. Mountbatten was the Patron of the Society of
Naval Research, later succeeded by Prince Philip; Prince Louis, the father, had
launched the Save the Victory Fund, an important arm of SNR.

304   Murfett, Malcolm, ed.   The First Sea Lords: From Fisher to
Mountbatten. Westport, CT: Praeger, 1995, 327 pp. A series of 18 essays and
scholarly analyses of the First Sea Lords of the Royal Navy, 1904-1959; the
essay on Mountbatten (pp. 265-282) by Geoffrey Till; an introductory essay by
Murfett; essay on Prince Louis of Battenberg (pp. 75-90) by John Hattendorf;
Mountbatten was First Sea Lord during a crucial period, the "age of
thermonuclear weapons"; Mountbatten cultivated friendships with Admirals
Arleigh Burke and Hyman Rickover of the U.S. Navy, leading to the adoption
by the Royal Navy of nuclear power for submarines and the Polaris missile.

305   Murphy, Ray Livingston. Last Viceroy: The Life and Times of Rear
Admiral the Earl Mountbatten of Burma. London: Jarrolds, 1948, 270 pp. A
biography of Mountbatten; chapters were entitled "Father of D-Day?" and "Pro-
Consul of Compromise"; covered up to 1947.

306   Nailor, Peter.   The Nassau Connection: The Organisation and
Management of the British Polaris Project. London: HMSO, 1988, 142 pp. A
study sponsored by the Ministry of Defence presenting the background and
details of the Nassau agreement between Prime Minister Macmillan and President
Kennedy; provided the British with the Polaris missile system for its submarines;
Mountbatten was involved in the process.

307   Navias, Martin S. Nuclear Weapons and British Strategic Planning,
1955-1958. Nuclear History Program # 1. Oxford: Clarendon, 1991, 269 pp.
A review of the making of nuclear strategy by the British government; included
the Defence White Paper of 1955 and Sandys White Paper of 1957.

308 -------. "The Sandys White Paper of 1957 and the Move to the British New Look: An Analysis of Nuclear Weapons, Conventional Force and Strategic Planning, 1955-1957." Ph.D. diss. London, 1989. The dissertation which was the basis for the previous entry.

309 Nelson, Hank. "'The Nips are Going for the Parker [pen]': The Prisoners Face Freedom." WARSOC, 3 (September 1985): 127-43. The story of Australian POWs throughout Southeast Asia; universial complaints about delays in the process of repatriation after the war ended; nickname for Mountbatten: "Linger Longer Louis"; most were freed in September and October 1945.

310 Olver, A.S.B. Outline of British Policy in East and Southeast Asia, 1945-May 1950. London: RIIA, 1950, 83 pp. A country-by-country overview sponsored by the Royal Institute of International Affairs; emphasis on trade and economic factors; Mountbatten was SAC SEAC during the eary months.

311 Owen, Charles. No More Heroes: The Royal Navy in the Twentieth Century: Anatomy of a Legend. London: Allen, 1975, 248 pp. A survey of prominent persons and events associated with the Royal Navy, 1900-1945, by a veteran; began with founding of the Navy League and the Fisher reforms of the first decade of the century; a summary of the administration and personnel; more on officers, e.g., colorful personalities and tensions between the executive and engineering branches.

312 Owen, Frank. The Campaign in Burma. London: HMSO, 1946, 175 pp. Profusely illustrated, an account of the campaign prepared for the SEAC by an army colonel; review of Wingate, Chindits, Stilwell, road construction, the Japanese "March on Delhi," and the battle of Kohima.

313 Owen, N.J. "'The Confusion of an Imperial Inheritance': The Labour Party and the Indian Problem, 1940-1947." Ph.D. diss. Oxford, 1993. A review of how the Labor Party of Great Britain treated the situation in India during and after the transfer of power; attitudes of the leaders about such things as the Cripps Mission, "Quit India" crisis, the decision for partition, and the subsequent violence.

314 Pack, Stanley W.C. The Battle for Crete. Sea Battles in Close-Up # 5. Annapolis: NIP; London: Allan, 1973, 144 pp. An account of the battle in a noted series, by a participant; the British situation deteriorated, stretching beyond the limits and culminating in a disaster; HMS KELLY was sunk during the battle.

315   Pakistan: Past and Present. London: Stacey, n.d., 288 pp. Folio size; published to commemorate the centenary of the birth of Jinnah, founder of Pakistan; Mountbatten contributed a recollection, "Jinnah: A Retrospect" (pp. 40-41).

316   Palmer, Alan W. Crowned Cousins: The Anglo-German Royal Connection. London: Weidenfeld; NY: Biblio, 1985, 1986, 265 pp. Re descendants of early seventeenth century German nobles, linking the British and German dynasties; the Hanovarian connection; the relationship ended with World War I; the Duke of Windsor, former Edward VIII, failed to revive the link when he flirted with Hitler; reference to Prince Louis of Battenberg and Mountbatten.

317   -------. Dictionary of the British Empire and Commonwealth. London: Murray, 1996, 412 pp. A reference guide on British imperial developments, up-to-the-minute, e.g., the latest members, # 52 and 53, Cameroon and Mozambique; Mountbatten included (p. 241).

318   Pandey, B.N. The Break-up of British India. Making of the Twentieth Century series. NY: Macmillan, 1969, 262 pp. From a brilliant series, concentrating on the several decades before the transfer and separation of India in 1947; partition was not inevitable, it created problems and solved none; chapter on "India Divided" (pp. 191-211), focused on the role of Mountbatten.

319   -------. South and South-East Asia, 1945-1979: Problems and Policies. Making of the Twentieth Century series. NY: St. Martin, 1980, 244 pp. Another in the impressive series; about the decolonisation and emergence of the large region of Asia; 14 countries arose with a population of 1.1 billion; Mountbatten was SAC SEAC during the early months.

320   Parker, John. Prince Philip: A Critical Biography. Alt. subtitle: His Secret Life. London: Sidgwick; NY: St. Martin, 1990, 280 pp. Described as the enigmatic husband of Queen Elizabeth II; many references to the uncle, Mountbatten, and the dynastic name of the royal family; Philip was from a line of German-Danish-Russian nobles whose father died bankrupt; much gossip and a cynical tone throughout; re the royal name: in 1959 Elizabeth agreed to change the name to Mountbatten-Windsor but Churchill and the Cabinet objected; a compromise: all descendants not "HRHs" would use Mountbatten-Windsor, the "Royals" would continue as the House of Windsor.

321   Parkes, Oscar. British Battleships, WARRIOR 1860 to VANGUARD 1950: A History of Design, Construction and Armaments. Foreword by Earl Mountbatten. London: Seeley, 1957, 1958, 1972, 1990, 701 pp. By the editor of Jane's Fighting Ships; included detailed schematic drawings among the 450 illustrations.

322 Patterson, A. Temple. The University of Southampton: A Centenary History of the Evolution and Developement of the University of Southampton, 1862-1962. Southampton: USH, 1962, 245 pp. A history of the university by a noted naval biographer; later the Broadlands Archive is transferred to the university library.

323 Pattinson, William. Mountbatten and the Men of the KELLY. London: Stephens, 1986, 216 pp. Foreword by Prince of Wales; preface by Philip Ziegler; by a journalist and veteran of destroyers; a memorial to the destroyer and to Mountbatten; about the organization, the KELLY Reunion Association; the copy in the Mountbatten library was signed by about 30 persons; Mountbatten personally wrote over 900 letters to KELLY survivors.

324 Payn, Graham. My Life with Noel Coward. NY: Applause, 1994. A memoir by a longtime companion and later manager of Coward's estate; called himself part of "the Family."

325 Philip, Duke of Edinburgh. "Lord Louis." NIPROC, 106 (February 1980): 26-35. By the uncle of Mountbatten; described a distinguised naval, military, and diplomatic career, above all, a dedicated navy man with 52 years service; Mountbatten specialized in signals and wireless telegraphy; oversaw the earliest plans for the Normandy invasion; article included 33 pictures, e.g., P.A. de Laszlo portrait of 1924.

326 Philips, C.H. and Wainwright, Mary D., eds. The Partition of India: Policies and Perspectives, 1935-1947. Cambridge: MIT, 1970, 607 pp. A series of 29 essays from seminars on partition conducted over 3 years; noted essayists included P.N.S. Mansergh and R.J. Moore; essays on Nehru, Gandhi, Jinnah, the Muslim League, Congress Party, and Mountbatten, the essay by H.V. Hudson (pp. 117-26); contended the personal influence of Mountbatten on the partition has been exaggerated; Mountbatten was reluctant to go to India, fearing it would jeapordize his naval career; he demanded guarantees; praise for Mountbatten and Lady Mountbatten for physical courage, especially exposure to crowds.

327 Phillips, Cecil E.L. and Hasler, H.G. Cockleshell Heroes. Foreword by Earl Mountbatten. London: Heinemann; Glasgow: Blackie; Boston: Little, Brown, 1956, 1960, 1961, 1971, 264 pp. A dramatic account, made into a film, of a single commando operation, 4 men who canoed into the Gironde estuary around Bordeaux destroying blockade runners.

328 -------. The Greatest Raid of All: An Account of the Famous World War II Commando Raid against Ships of the German Navy. Foreword by Earl Mountbatten. London: Heinemann; Boston: Little, Brown, 1958, 1960, 306 pp. A series of raids operated by COHQ, some using X-craft, small submarines; included the St. Nazaire raid, March 1942.

329 -------. Springboard to Victory: The Battle of Kohima Ridge and the Burma Campaign. London: Heinemann, 1966, 256 pp. The key battle in the second Burma campaign; a detailed description of all phases of the battle, the beginning of the end of the Japanese forces.

330 Pierre, Andrew J. Nuclear Politics: The British Experience with an Independent Strategic Force, 1939-1970. London: Oxford UP, 1972, 386 pp. A perceptive study of the creation and development of a nuclear program by the British; they were first to decide to build an A-bomb, in 1941, and then joined the Manhattan Project; later cooperation with delays and problems after the war; Mountbatten was instrumental in acquisition of nuclear powered submarine technology and the Polaris missile.

331 Poolman, Kenneth. The KELLY: HMS KELLY, the Story of Mountbatten's Warship. Foreword by Earl Mountbatten. London: Kimber; NY: Norton, 1954, 1955, 1974, 1980, 238 pp. H history of the short life of HMS KELLY, Mountbatten as captain; Mountbatten's foreword recalled his life in the navy, beginning when he was 16 years old, service in 20 ships; the one that stands out was KELLY; "I was the only commander she had" (p. 6).

332 Post, Laurens van der. The Admiral's Baby. London: Murray, 1996, 322 pp. Van der Post died in December 1996, 90 years old; one of a series of volumes of memoirs; acted as a prominent British representative during and after the war in Indonesia; he was a POW there and remained after repatriation to facilitate the return of the Dutch; increasingly upset with the insensitivity of the returning Dutch colonials; on mission to Mountbatten in Ceylon to report his concerns, thence to the Attlee government, and finally to the Dutch government, hoping to persuade to use restraint; the nationalist revolted against the Dutch, beginning 3 years of war.

333 Prather, Russel E. Easy into Burma. Private pub., 1977, 92 pp. A paperback edition about the 1st Air Commando Group during the Burma campaign; Wingate initially was unsuccessful in operations against the Japanese due to lack of supplies and support; Wingate invited by Churchill to Quebec Conference; support and cooperation from Mountbatten; later LRPG operations.

334   Pratt, Marjorie Minna, Countess of Brecknoch, ed.   <u>Edwina Mountbatten: Her Life in Pictures</u>. London: Macdonald, 1961, 112 pp. Foreword by Sir Arthur Bryant; folio size with many illustrations; published shortly after the death of Lady Mountbatten; Bryant mourned her death: "she had it all, rare good looks, charm, a vast fortune, a dazzling inheritance, and a brilliant and happy marriage" (p. 3); a short introduction by Lady Brecknoch and 100 pages of photos.

335   "Raid on Saint-Nazaire." <u>After the Battle</u>, 59 (May 1988): 1-23. The only large drydock on the Atlantic seaboard which could hold the German battleships, <u>TIRPITZ</u> and <u>BISMARCK</u> was at St. Nazaire; OPERATION CHARIOT planned by COHQ, 28 March 1942; the drydock was effectively destroyed for the duration.

336   Ramsey, W.G. <u>Dieppe Then and Now</u>. <u>Battle of Britain Prints International</u>. London: After the Battle, 1993, 1994, 32 pp. A unique format: b/w photos of the battle and aftermath, e.g., British POWs being marched through the streets, the "Then"; then blank pages where present-day photos taken by the reader could be inserted, the "Now"; a kind of battlefield tour book; "the raid was an unmitigated disaster" (p. 3).

337   Rasor, Eugene L. <u>The Battle of Jutland: A Bibliography</u>. <u>Bibliographies of Battles and Leaders</u> series # 7. Westport: Greenwood, 1992, 190 pp.   A comprehensive annotated bibliography with 528 entries and an extensive historiographical essay on this important naval battle in World War I; Mountbatten reported aboard <u>HMS LION</u>, flagship of Admiral David Beatty, several weeks after the battle.

338   -------. <u>British Naval History since 1815: A Guide to the Literature</u>. <u>Military History Bibliographies</u> series # 13. NY: Garland, 1990, 864 pp. A comprehensive survey of the literature about British naval and maritime history since 1815, focusing on publications since 1960; 3125 entries and 517 pp. of historiographical narrative.

339   -------. <u>The China-Burma-India Campaign, 1941-1945: Historiography and Annotated Bibliography</u>. <u>Bibliographies of Battles and Leaders</u> series # 22. Westport, CT: Greenwood, 1998, 240 pp.   A comprehensive annotated bibliography with 1613 entries and an extensive historiographical essay on this, one of the three major theaters of the Asian/Pacific War, the theater commanded by Mounbatten, 1943 until after the war and until some stability was established; a summary of the extensive literature dealing with C-B-I.

340 -------. General Douglas MacArthur, 1880-1964: Historiography and Annotated Bibliography. Bibliographies of Battles and Leaders series # 12. Westport: Greenwood, 1994, 260 pp. A comprehensive annotated bibliography with 760 entries and an extensive historiographical essay on MacArthur, among other things, SAC Southwest Pacific Theater during the war; Mountbatten visited MacArthur in the Philippines and corresponded with him on occasion.

341 -------. The Southwest Pacific Campaign, 1941-1945: Historiography and Annotated Bibliography. Bibliographies of Battles and Leaders series # 19. Westport: Greenwood, 1996, 297 pp. A comprehensive annotated bibliography with 1535 entries and an extensive historiographical essay on one of the three theaters of the Asian/Pacific war, this one commanded by General Douglas MacArthur; at the end of the war, a large territorial section of this theater in Southeast Asia was transferred to C-B-I, the theater commanded by Mountbatten.

342 Reed, Bruce and Williams, Geoffrey. Denis Healey and the Policies of Power. London: Sidgwick, 1971, 286 pp. Healey was Labor Minister of Defence in the Wilson government; Mountbatten was Chief of the Defence Staff but was planning to retire in several months; Healey conducted a defence review and decided to cancel CVA-O1, a super aircraft carrier; a bitter interservice struggle ensued between the navy and air force; Mountbatten and Solly Zuckerman disagreed but Mountbatten remained strangely quiet, still a mystery.

343 Rees, Wyn. "The 1957 Sandys White Paper: New Priorities in British Defence Policy." JSTRSTU, 12 (June 1989): 215-29. Duncan Sandys, Minister of Defence under the Macmillan government, issued a White Paper provided for drastic cuts in the budgets of all three services, after Suez; the air force was favored and the nuclear program would be air based; conventional warfare was downgraded.   Research Guide to European Historical Biography, 1450-Present. 4 vols. Wash: Beacham, 1992, 2270 pp. Ed. by James Moncure; a biographical dictionary with 197 subjects; entry on Mountbatten by W. Robert Houston (III., pp. 1450-57); "perhaps only Douglas MacArthur comes close to equalling Mountbatten's many roles and the vigor with which he played them" (p. 1452).

344 Reyburn, Wallace. Glorious Chapter. Alt. titles: Rehearsal for Invasion and Dawn Landing. London: Brown; London: Harrap, 1943, 1958, 160 pp. By the historian of Rugby; a wartime best seller, touted as the only eye-witness account of Dieppe; ironically, the author later repudiated the "rehearsal for invasion" claim and stirred up some acrimony, notably with the Canadian commander, Hughes-Hallett, in the Sunday Telegraph.

345   Reynolds, Quentin. <u>Dress Rehearsal: The Story of Dieppe</u>. NY: Random, 1943, 278 pp. A contemporaneous account by a war correspondent, 13 untitled chapters on the Dieppe raid, "9 hours of hell"; nevertheless, concluded that all had gone well and that Mountbatten was "a remarkable man," perhaps comparable to Stonewall Jackson (p. viii)

346   Rhodes James, Robert. <u>Anthony Eden</u>. London: Weidenfeld; NY: McGraw, 1986, 1987, 679 pp. A semi-official biography which access to the Eden papers and government documents opened after 30 years; a third was on the Suez crisis; apologetics for Eden; blamed Cabinet and military, including Mountbatten whom Eden claimed had lied and falsified history.

347   Rizvi, Gowher. <u>Linlithgow and India: A Study of British Policy and Political Impasse in India, 1936-1943</u>. Royal Historical Society Studies series # 13. London: RHS, 1978, 271 pp. Lord Linlithgow was Viceroy of India once removed before Mountbatten; continued attempts to resolve the anticipated crisis over the transfer of power; Cripps Mission failed and problems with Jinnah and the Muslim League increased; Linlithgow was accused of perpetuating the "divide and rule" approach.

348   Roberts, Hugh A. "Royal Retreat." <u>British Heritage</u>, 13 (August 1992): 32-36. Re Frogmore House, within Home Park, Windsor Castle, a little-known royal residence; opened to the public in 1990; Mountbatten was born in it.

349   Rockwell, Theodore. <u>The Rickover Effect: How One Man Made a Difference</u>. Annapolis: NIP, 1992, 411 pp. Biography of Admiral Hyman G. Rickover, creator of nuclear power reactors for American warships by an associate; at the request of Mountbatten, Rickover demonstrated the power plant and approved the program providing American reactor technology to the Royal Navy.

350   Romanus, Charles F. and Sunderland, Riley. <u>The China-Burma-India Theater</u> <u>The U.S. Army in World War II</u>. 3 vols. Wash: GPO, 1953-1959, 1966, 1442 pp. The official U.S. Army history of C-B-I; this official history series, about 100 volues total, has been much praised for scholarship and critical analysis; concentrated on the Stilwell mission, the command structure, and American operations, especially in China and Burma; Stilwell was Chief of Staff to Mountbatten, among other offices; he called Mountbatten "Glamor Boy" and worse.

351   Romanus, Charles F. and Sunderland, Riley, eds. <u>Stilwell's Personal File: China-Burma-India, 1942-1944</u>. 5 vols. Wilmington: Scholarly, 1976,

2610 pp. A massive primary source, an extensive collection of papers and documents associated with the controversial mission; very informative.

352   Rooney, D. David. <u>Burma Victory: Imphal, Kohima, and the Chindit Issue, March 1944 to May 1945</u>. London: Arms, 1992, 1993, 208 pp. By a military academy professor; an apologist for Wingate and the Chindit operations in the Burma campaign; OPERATION THURSDAY contributed significantly to the overall Allied victory over the Japanese.

353   --------. "A Grave Injustice: Wingate and the Establishment." <u>HISTOD</u>, 44 (March 1994): 11-13. Orde Wingate formed and commanded LRPGs, the Chindits, during the Burma campaign and was killed in a plane crash, March 1944; Rooney was an apologist; Wingate and the Chindits were severely criticized in the official British history of the war, the volume by Woodburn Kirby; Mountbatten called Wingate a pain in the neck but later cited the Chindits as the best example in the war of cooperation of the various services and Allies (pp.12-13).

354   Rose, Kenneth. <u>King George V</u>. London: Weidenfeld, 1983, 528 pp. A biography of the British king; Mountbatten was cited frequently.

355   Roskill, Stephen W. "The Dieppe Raid and the Question of German Foreknowledge: A Study in Historical Responsibility." <u>JRUSI</u>, 109 (February 1964): 27-31. In a letter to <u>Daily Telegraph</u>, 9 September 1963, David Irving claimed the Germans were warned weeks before the Dieppe raid; Roskill, the official naval historian of the war, denied the claim by Irving; indeed, the docuents recently available in Germany proved Germany was <u>NOT</u> warned; the debate continued in correspondence to <u>Daily Telegraph</u>, <u>Evening Standard</u>, and <u>Der Spiegel</u>; Mountbatten denied the Germans knew of the plan in a CBC broadcast in 1962.

356   --------. <u>The War at Sea, 1939-1945</u>. <u>The Official Naval History of World War II</u>. 3 vols. in 4 books. London: HMSO, 1954-1961, 2100 pp. The much acclaimed official British history of the naval war, including coverage of American naval operations in the Pacific; claimed access to all pertinent documents.

357   Ross, Al. <u>The Destroyer CAMPBELTOWN</u>. <u>Anatomy of the Ship</u>. Annapolis: NIP, 1990, 128 pp. An account of the destroyer used to blow up the drydock at St. Nazaire; it was one of the 50 American destroyers, <u>USS BUCHANAN</u>, in the destroyers for bases deal.

358   Royle, Trevor. <u>Orde Wingate: Irregular Soldier</u>. London: Weidenfeld, 1995, 368 pp. A new biography of Wingate who has been the object of a continuing controversy among British military historians, including the official history which treated Wingate negatively; access to Wingate and family papers; Wingate had been equally innovative in operations in Palestine and Ethiopia previously; he combined the concepts of Stonewall Jackson and Lawrence of Arabia; Churchill, Mountbatten, FDR, and Wavell all agreed Wingate was one of the few men of genius in the war.

359   Sbrega, John J. "Anglo-American Relations and the Selection of Mountbatten as Supreme Allied Commander, Southeast Asia." <u>MA</u>, 46 (October 1982): 139-45. The appointent of Mountbatten was a factor in Anglo-American relations; the British wanted to gain more influence and upgrade a neglected theater while the Americans feared neo-colonialism; the U.S. was optimistic about potential for war expansion in China while the British were sceptical; several candidates were mentioned: Air Marshal Tedder and Admiral A.B. Cunningham; it was the Americans who first suggested Mountbatten and Churchill reacted enthusiastically; Mountbatten feared the appointment would jeopardize his naval career.

360   Seervai, Hormasji M. <u>Partition of India: Legend and Reality</u>. Bombay: Emmenem, 1989, 1990, 245 pp. By an Indian official, dedicated to the millions of Indians who became victims at the time of the separation; an appraisal based on publication of government documents and memoirs of participants; chapters on Mountbatten's Viceroyalty and his responsibility for the massacres and migrations in the Punjab (pp. 114-67); called it the "great betrayal."

361   Sherwani, Latif A. <u>The Partition of India and Mountbatten</u>. Karachi: Council, 1986, 205 pp. The Pakistani perspcetive about the transfer of power, the separation, and the role of Mountbatten.

362   Shuckburgh, Evelyn. <u>Descent to Suez: Diaries, 1951-1956</u>. London: Weidenfeld; NY: Norton, 1986, 1987, 390 pp. Ed. by John Charmley; the edited diaries of an "insider," an intimate of Eden's and official in the Middle East office of the Foreign Office; recounted decisions and policies which led to Suez; many mistakes and much confusion were documented; noted deteriorating health of Eden; a letter-writer concluded: "Suez was conceived in deceit and arrested in pusillanimity" (p. 366).

363   Simpson, John. <u>The Independent Nuclear State: The U.S., Britain, and the Military Atom</u>. NY: St. Martin; London: Macmillan, 1983, 1985, 353 pp. A historical review of the development of atomic energy, weapons, and propulsion; much Anglo-American cooperation was involved; included the nuclear alliance and acquisiton of Polaris.

364 Simpson, Michael, ed. The Somerville Papers: Selections from the Private and Official Correspondence of Admiral of the Fleet Sir James Somerville, GCB, GBE. Aldershot: Gower, 1995, 721 pp. Assisted by John Somerville; the published papers of the naval chief of staff under Mountbatten; Somerville was one of several admirals whom Churchill had criticized; friction between Mountbatten and Somerville ensued at SEAC and he was recalled and assigned to Washington as British Admiralty delegate.

365 Slim, Sir William. Defeat into Victory. London: Cassell; NY: McKay; NY: Papermac, 1956, 1961, 1987, 550 pp. By Field Marshall Viscount Slim, commander of the 14th Army which defeated the Japanese in the Burma campaign; Mountbatten called Slim the best general of the war; a memoir of defeat and victory, very informative; much praised as a war memoir.

366 Smith, Charles. Lord Mountbatten: His Butler's Story. Alt. title: Fifty Years with Mountbatten. London: Sidgwick; NY: Stein, 1980, 176 pp. Born in 1908, Smith's service began as footman to Lady Mountbatten in 1930, later as valet and butler to Mountbatten, retiring in 1974; recollections of numerous episodes associated with Mountbatten.

367 Smith, Simon C. British Relations with the Malay Rulers from Decentralization to Malayan Independence, 1930-1957. South-East Asian Historical Monograph. NY: Oxford UP, 1995, 184 pp. A recent overview of the colonial status and decolonization of Malaya; Mountbatten was SAC SEAC at the time of the liberation from Japanese occupation for several months thereafter.

368 Smurthwaite, David, ed. The Forgotten War: The British Army in the Far East, 1941-1945. London: Army Museum, 1992, 207 pp. Folio size with a series essays by noted historians, e.g., Brian Bond, James Lunt, and Brian Holden Reid; on the occasion of the 50th anniversary of the fall of Singapore, a new permanent exhibition was opened to commemorate the 14th Army, the "forgotten army" and its campaigns were the "forgotten war"

369 Snyder, William P. The Politics of British Defence Policy, 1945-1962. Columbus: Ohio State UP, 1964, 1965, 296 pp. For the Mershon Center for National Security; an overview of how Great Britain adjusted its defence policies for two decades after the war; a series of crises led to many changes and decreased forces.

370   -------. "The Politics of British Defence Policy, 1951-1961." Ph.D. diss. Princeton, 1963, 419 pp. The dissertation upon which the previous entry was based.

371   "Sources for Research." Pamphlet of Special Collections Division, The Hartley Library, University of Southampton. Southampton: U Southampton, 1992, 10 pp. A brief description of the Special Collections Division, 850,000 books and over 2 million other items such as diaries, personal and official papers, and media materials; included the Broadlands Archives.

372   Spector, Ronald H. "Allied Intelligence and Indochina, 1943-1945." PACHISREV, 51 (February 1982): 23-50. An aspect of Anglo-American relations at the end of the war; American intelligence agencies, e.g., OSS, USN, and U.S. Army, provided aid to anti-colonial rebels, something that upset the British who aided in restoration of colonial French authorities; Mountbatten provided for 26 sorties into Indochina which upset American authorities on the scene; July 1945 decision to divide Indochina at 16 degrees North and allocate responsibilities to the China theater and SEAC theater.

373   -------. Eagle against the Sun: The American War with Japan. NY: Free, 1984, 1985, 1987, 605 pp. A standard and impressive history of the Asian/Pacific War utilizing declassified intelligence sources and the latest literature; despite the title/subtitle, full coverage of C-B-I; the war ended Western domination in the Far East and the Japanese facilitated the process; apologist for two-pronged advance across the Pacific, appeasing armed service competitive tendencies; C-B-I covered in the chapter, "A Hell of a Beating" (pp. 324-45); China envisioned as future great power and received aid on a massive scale, all of this a basis for Anglo-American disagreement; extensive coverage of intelligence and guerrilla operations within C-B-I.

374   Spoto, Donald. The Decline and Fall of the House of Windsor. NY: Simon, 1996, 480 pp. A sensationalized account of the Windsors; emphasis on royal scandals and media stars; Mountbatten was partial to the latter.

375   Squire, Clifford W. "Britain and the Transfer of Power in Indonesia, 1945-1946." Ph.D. diss. London, 1979. Rare coverage of the postwar disposition of the Dutch colony and British participation; included the area under the responsibility of Mountbatten.

376   Stacey, C.P. "The Raid on Dieppe." MILREV, 29 (May and June 1949): 7-18 and 26-37. Excerpts from the official Canadian army history of the war; began with the appointment of Mountbatten to replace Keyes as COHQ

director, followed by the planning and execution of the Dieppe raid; an issue very sensitive among Canadians.

377 ------. Official History of the Canadian Army in the Second World War. 3 vols. Ottawa: Printer, 1955-1966. The official history of Canadian Army operations during the war; the pertinent volume is the first which included the Dieppe raid, a very controversial episode in Canadian military history.

378 Stannard, Martin. Evelyn Waugh. 2 vols. NY: Norton, 1986-1992, 1060 pp. The definitive biography of Evelyn Waugh; another example of a case where Mountbatten sought out contacts with celebrities.

379 Steers, H.J.T. "The Higher Direction of Combined Operations in the United Kingdom from Dunkirk to Pearl Harbor." Ph.D. diss. London, 1982. Included background and the early months of the Mountbatten regime at COHQ.

380 Stephen, Martin. The Fighting Admirals: British Admirals of the Second World War. Annapolis: NIP, 1991, 217 pp. A work developed by a prominent Naval historian to rehabilitate certain British admirals, e.g., Thomas Phillips, A.B. Cunningham, Dudley Pound, and James Somerville; coverage of the Mountbatten-Somerville clash, "very stormy relations" (pp. 169-73); e.g., Somerville accused Mountbatten of addressing crews of his ships without his knowledge; aspects of the complicated command structure of SEAC and interventions by Winston Churchill.

381 Sternlicht, Sanford V. C.S. Forester. Twayne's English Authors series. Boston: Twayne, 1981, 177 pp. Forester, 1899-1966, became a famous naval novelist/historian, e.g., the Hornblower series and the BISMARCK chase; approached by the Mountbatten family to write the official biography; Forester's death meant a shift to Ziegler.

382 Stilwell, Joseph W. The Stilwell Papers. NY: Sloan; NY: McFadden; NY: DaCapo, 1948, 1962, 1991, 1992, 375 pp. Ed. by Theodore White; dedicated to Madame Sun Yat-sen; from the diaries, notes, and letters of Stilwell (1883-1946); the papers are located at the Hoover Institution at Stanford; clearly demonstrated the feistiness and Anglophobia of "Vinegar Joe," who loved China and despised "the Peanut," Chiang; Stilwell was Chief of Staff to Mountbatten.

383 Strange, Joseph L. "Cross-Channel Attack, 1942: The British Rejection of OPERATION SLEDGEHAMMER and the Cherbourg Alternative." Ph.D. diss. Maryland, 1984, 498 pp. Enlightening on the making of Allied strategy and final planning for the Normandy invasion in June 1944; during 1941-1942,

General Marshall came to Britain to make plans for the invasion of continental Europe, favoring an operation in 1942; Mountbatten suggested Cherbourg; after much debate and opposition of Churchill and General Brooke, the invasion of North Africa was decided upon.

384   Strong, Charles L. Common-sense Therapy for Horses' Injuries. Foreword by Earl Mountbatten. London: Faber, 1956, 196 pp. Mountbatten urged Strong to write this instruction manuel on the treatment of injuries to polo-ponies.

385   -------. Horse Injuries: Common-sense Therapy of Muscles and Joints for the Layman. Foreword by Earl Mountbatten. London: Faber, 1967, 118 pp. An instruction manual for treatment of specific types of injuries to horses, especially polo-ponies.

386   Strutton, Bill and Pearson, Michael. The Secret Invaders. Foreword by Earl Mountbatten. London: Hodder, 1958, 286 pp. Re the formation, training, and operations of Combined Operations Pilotage Parties (COPP), a special force of swimmers to make preparations for amphibious invasions, e.g., Normandy and in the Far East.

387   Sweetman, John, ed. Sword and Mace: Twentieth-Century Civil-Military Relations in Britain. London: Brassey, 1986, 189 pp. A series of essays by experts from the military academy at Sandhurst; about relationships between the army and society, e.g., the creation of the Ministry of Defence, an important initiative credited to Mountbatten, that essay by the editor, Sweetman.

388   Swettenham, John, ed. Valiant Men: Canada's Victoria Cross and George Cross Winners. Foreword by Earl Mountbatten. Toronto: Hakkert, 1973, 234 pp. The frontispiece, a photo of Mountbatten in the uniform of Admiral of the Fleet; the first book on Canadian winners of these most prestigious military awards, e.g., for valor in such camapigns as the Crimea, India, South Africa, and the two World Wars.

389   Swinson, Arthur. Mountbatten. Ballatine Illustrated History of World War II: War Leader series # 4. NY: Ballantine; London: Pan, 1971, 1973, 160 pp. Introduction by Barrie Pitt; a biography in a series of popular histories and biographies associated with the war; Swinson died in 1971; many illustrations; topics include HMS KELLY, Dieppe, Supremo, Burma, India; noted the "gross injustice" to Mountbatten's father in World War I.

390   Talbot, I.A. "Mountbatten and the Partition of India: A Rejoinder."
HISTORY, 69 (February 1984): 29-35. A response to the article by Y.
Krishnan which blamed Mountbatten for Muslim-Hindu-Sikh violence after
partition; enormous pressures were being exerted on Mountbatten and British
authority was weakening, so something must be done more quickly than the
earlier announced date of June 1948; thus the decision by Mountbatten was best
under the circumstances.

391   Tarling, Nicholas. The Fall of Imperial Britain in South-East Asia.
South-East Asian Historical Monograph series. NY: Oxford UP, 1993, 240 pp.
An ambitious survey and analysis of British policies in Southeast Asia over two
centuries until decolonization; chapter 5 on World War II (pp. 130-69) was
pertinent to the role of Mountbatten in Burma, Malaya, and India.

392   -------. "Lord Mountbatten and the Return of Civil Government to
Burma." JI&CH, 11 (January 1983): 197-226. Mountbatten regarded the fact
that an independent Burma did not join the Commonwealth as his "first failure";
he regretted that the return of the Governor, Sir Reginald Dorman-Smith, was
approved by him; from hindsight, Mountbatten should have rejected his efforts
and cooperated more with the nationalist leaders; Tarling doubted if anything
could have been done to keep Burma in the Commonwealth.

393   -------. The Sun Never Sets: An Historical Essay on Britain and Its
Place in the World. London: Oriental, 1986, 152 pp. A review and rationale
of the twentieth-century imperial and Commonwealth history.

394   Taylor, A.J.P. Beaverbrook. London: Hamilton; NY: Simon, 1972,
729 pp. This powerful press baron and government minister was a persistent
critic of Mountbatten.

395   Teed, Peter. Dictionary of Twentieth-Century History, 1914-1990.
Oxford: UP, 1992, 528 pp.   One of a number of such dictionaries and
encyclopedias; most historically significant features of the century, Mountbatten
included (p. 315).

396   Terraine, John. L'amiral Mountbatten: Sa vie et son epoque. Paris:
Presses, 1969, 212 pp. A French-language edition of the next entry.

397   -------. The Life and Times of Lord Mountbatten Foreword by Earl
Mountbatten. London: Hutchinson; NY: Holt, 1968, 1980, 212 pp. The
biography of Mountbatten to support the 13-part TV documentary which

Mountbatten himself narrated; a postscript was added the the 1980 edition, details of the assassination; there were 2 other IRA bombings that day.

398   Terry, Thurzal Q. Strangers in Their Land: C-B-I Bombardier, 1939-1945. Manhattan: Sunflower, 1992, 272 pp. By the bombardier of a B-24 of the 10th Air Force; a chapter (pp. 65-71) on Mountbatten, "El Supremo," an extremely popular and capable commander skillful at smoothing Anglo-American relations; participated in a bomber raid on Bangkok in March 1945.

399   Thomas, David A. "The Importance of Commando Operations in Modern Warfare, 1939-1982." JCOMTEMHIS, 18 (October 1983): 689-717. An overview of the origins and development of commando operations, self-contained acts mounted by self-sufficient forces within enemy territory; the British, Germans, and Russias used them extensively in the war; for the British there were SAS, SBS, SOG, and LRPG.

400   -------. Nazi Victory: Crete, 1941. NY: Stein, 1972, 1973, 228 pp. A chronicle of the important campaign, the German attack on Greece and then Crete, driving the British forces out; HMS KELLY was sunk in the latter campaign; 7 other destroyers and 3 cruisers were also sunk.

401   Thomas, Hugh. The Suez Affair. Alt. title: Suez. London: Weidenfeld; NY: Harper, 1967, 261 pp. One of the best early accounts of the operation and crisis, before many documents became available to researchers; a expedition in which there were no victors.

402   Thompson, Julian. The Lifeblood of War: Logistics in Armed Conflict. London: Brassey, 1991, 418 pp. By a general in the British Army, veteran of the Falklands/Malvinas campaign; case studies, including the Burma campaign of World War II (pp. 51-104), calling it the logistic triumph of the war; Mountbatten, as SAC SEAC, ordered the campaign to continue through the monsoon season, an unprecedented move; also cited LRPGs.

403   Thorne, Christopher G. Allies of a Kind: The United States, Britain, and the War against Japan, 1941-1945. New York: Oxford UP, 1978, 772 pp. A prize-winning assessment of Anglo-American relations and actions in the Asian/Pacific War; disposition of empires was a major issue, also racial and cultural antagonisms; plus examination of the broadest political and strategic issues; there were many differences between the Americans and the British, and they won the war; Thorne believed Churchill wanted a true community of interest but that was not achieved partly because of Stilwell, Hornbeck, an American advisor, and Mountbatten.

404   -------. The Issue of War: States, Societies, and the Far Eastern Conflict, 1941-1945. Alt. title: The Far Eastern War. London: Oxford UP; NY: Unwin, 1985, 1988, 384 pp. The sequel to the previous entry with more emphasis on the Asian states and societies, e.g., the Dutch, French, Australians, New Zealanders, plus the British and Americans.

405   Tinker, Hugh, ed. Burma: The Struggle for Independence, 1944-1948. 2 vols. London: HMSO, 1983-1984. An exhaustive study of the transfer of power in Burma by a distinguished scholar of South and Southeast Asia.

406   -------. Experiment with Freedom: India and Pakistan, 1947. Chatham House Essays # 16. NY: Oxford UP, 1967, 175 pp. For the Royal Institute of International Affairs, a distinguished international think tank; reviewed events and policies leading to the transfer and separation; Mountbatten was portrayed as an amiable fellow, "the modern prince," (p. 90) who did a difficult job well.

407   -------. Men Who Overturned Empires: Fighters, Dreamers, and Schemes. Madison: UWiscP, 1987, 287 pp. From a series of 8 public lectures on major personalities involved, including Jinnah, Nehru, Aung Sang, U Nu, and Ho Chi Minh; they were responsible for the transfer of power and the end of empire.

408   -------. The Union of Burma: A Study of the First Years of Idependence. NY: Oxford UP, 1957, 1961, 1967, 438 pp. For the Royal Institute of International Affairs with several editions; a scholarly survey of the transfer of power.

409   Tiratsoo, Nick, ed. The Attlee Years. NY: Pinter, 1991, 224 pp. A series of essays on major issues which faced the government, 1945-1951, 2 concerning India and defense implications. Informative in that British defense and security factors directly affected the transfer of power in India for several reasons national service of British young men reduced from 18 to 12 months. Mountbatten pointed out the consequences on security policies including forces in India. Troops currently in India must come home earlier, which meant it would be impossible to hold on to India longer, thus the accelerated withdrawal, instead of June 1948, August 1947.

410   Trenowden, Ian. Operations Most Secret: S.O.E., the Malayan Theatre. Foreword by Earl Mountbatten. London: Kimber; Bristol: Crecy, 1978, 1994, 231 pp. An account of special operations in the Far East, especially Malaya; Group B, Force 136 under SEAC, infiltrated areas of Japanese occupation, usually by submarine, British and Dutch; at least 371 personnel were inserted by this group alone and over 3000 guerrillas were armed.

411   Tuchman, Barbara W. <u>Stilwell and the American Experience in China, 1911-1945</u>. NY: Macmillan, 1970, 1971, 636. The standard biography of Stilwell, Deputy Commander, SEAC; winner of Tuchman's second Pulitzer Prize; emphasis on the career of Stilwell in China, complex and controversial; he was recalled by FDR on October 1944, partly to appease Chiang Kai-shek.

412   Villa, Brian Loring. "Mountbatten, the British Chiefs of Staff, and Approval of the Dieppe Raid." <u>JMILHIS</u>, 54 (April 1990): 201-26. Villa was critical of the account of the Dieppe raid in the Ziegler biography; too accepting of the Mountbatten version and Mountbatten suffered from "obsessive defensiveness" (p. 204); concluded Mountbatten revived the planning and executed the Dieppe raid without permission or approval; included response from Ziegler, who rejected the thesis.

413   -------. <u>Unauthorized Action: Mountbatten and the Dieppe Raid</u>. NY: Oxford UP, 1989, 330 pp. By a Canadian professor of political science; received an award from the American Historical Association, 1990; the book stimulated numerous reviews and much comment; thesis: that the specific operation formulated by Mountbatten as Commander, COHQ, carried out in August 1942, was never officially approved, that the execution of the plan was a horrible disaster, and that the operation taught no lessons not already learned; noted the vendetta carried out against Mountbatten by Beaverbrook; Villa was critical of Mountbatten for lack of experience, vanity, exploitation of the royal connection, and for untruths; cynical and supercilious tone throughout; appendix at end: "Why Governments Do What They Should Not Do" (pp. 248-63); several gaffs, e.g., Mountbatten doing an interview in 1982 and the invasion in 1942 of North America

414   Warner, Oliver. <u>Admiral of the Fleet: The Life of Sir Charles Lambe</u>. Intro. by Earl Mountbatten. London: Sidgwick, 1969, 224 pp. Foreword by Sir Steven Runciman; biography of Lambe (1900-1960), friend, colleague, and 1st Sea Lord after Mountbatten.

415   Warner, Philip. <u>Auchinleck: The Lonely Soldier</u>. London: Buchan, 1981, 300 pp. A biography of this army general who was commander of British forces in India, 1942 until after Mountbatten departed.

416   Watson, Francis. "Gandhi and the Viceroys." <u>HISTOD</u>, 8 (February 1958): 88-97. The contacts and conflicts between Gandhi and 8 viceroys, the last of which was Mountbatten; Gandhi returned to India in 1915 and remained a force in Indian politics until his assassination in 1948; Mountbatten inverviewed with him 6 times, with "uninhibited friendliness."

417   Wavell, Archibald, Earl Wavell. <u>Wavell: The Viceroy's Journal</u>. London: Oxford UP, 1973, 544 pp. Ed. by Penderel Moon; Field Marshal Earl Wavell (1883-1950); the Viceroy immediately before Mountbatten; the original consisted of 11 vols., a day-by-day description, 1943-1947, in his own handwriting; informative on the many problems faced and the magnitude of the situation.

418   Werstein, Irving. <u>The Supremo: Lord Louis Mountbatten and the Testing of Democracy</u>. Phila: Smith, 1971, 143 pp. Juvenile literature; Weinstein died in 1971; a biography of the great-grandson of Queen Victoria, one of the century's most colorful and productive leaders; noted role in education: President of the International Council of United World Colleges.

419   Wheeler, Nicholas J. "The Role Played by the British Chiefs of Staff Committee in the Evolution of Britain's Nuclear Weapons Planning and Policy-Making, 1945-1955." Ph.D. diss. Southampton, 1988. Mountbatten has become 1st Sea Lord at the end of this decade under study; he helped formulate the nuclear weapons policy, later instrumental in acquiring Polaris missiles.

420   Wheeler-Bennett, John W. <u>The Life of George VI</u>. Alt. title: <u>King George VI: His Life and Reign</u>. London: Macmillan; NY: St. Martin, 1958, 891 pp. The authoritative biography, brother to Edward VIII, a solid but dull king; coverage of Mountbatten and his life.

421   <u>Where Great Adventures Start</u>. Intro. by Earl Mountbatten. Southampton: private pamphlet, 1970. Ed. by Arthur Jeffery; "published in memory of the Pilgrim Fathers who sailed in the <u>MAYFLOWER</u> from Southampton, 350 years ago (1620-1970). . . . Southampton's own story of adventures that shaped the history of the world"; Mountbatten described the original voyage, departing Southampton 15 August and arriving at Plymouth 26 December 1620, 102 settlers; a series of essays.

422   Whitaker, Denis and Whitaker, Shelagh. <u>Dieppe: Tragedy to Triumph</u>. Toronto: McGraw; London: Cooper, 1992, 387 pp. By a general, a veteran of the Dieppe raid, and his wife; a 50th anniversary commemoration of OPERATION JUBILEE, the tragic tactical failure; the controversy continues; reviewed the literature; Whitaker claimed he had captured a German who admitted anticipation of the attack; "Mountbatten ordered him to sit down--

Mountbatten did not believe Germany was forewarned" (p. xv); the "triumph": Eisenhower, Churchill, Alanbrooke, Marshall, and King all praised Mountbatten and COHQ for providing so many lessons learned for the Normandy invasion, June 1944; Whitaker agreed and was convinced the raid was supported by all authorities and the Germans had no advanced warning; all Canadians should be proud; the disputes and debate continued.

423 Whitehead, William and Macartney-Filgate, Terence. Dieppe, 1942: Echoes of Disaster. NY: St. Martin; Toronto: Personal; Glasgow: Drew, 1979, 1980, 1982, 187 pp. Another account of the Dieppe raid, this one quite curious; a picture book similar to a scrapbook associated with 2 CBC documentaries; cynical, badgering, and shrill criticism; the fight was "doomed from the start . . .and the echoes. . .can still be heard. . .chills the hearts of an entire generation of Canadians" (p. 2-3); 200 veterans interviewed.

424 Willmott, H.P. Grave of a Dozen Schemes: British Naval Planning and the War against Japan, 1943-1945. Annapolis: NIP; Shrewsbury: Airlife, 1995, 316 pp. A study with illustrations of the planning, preparation, and operations of the British fleet in the Asian/Pacific War; a full year of debate and planning ensued; many problems were encountered; Mountbatten was SAC SEAC.

425 -------. "Grave of a Dozen Schemes: The British Search for a Naval Strategy for the War against Japan, 1943-1944." Ph.D. diss. Oxford, 1991. The dissertation upon which the previous entry was based.

426 Wilson, Sir James. "Dieppe: Vindication." AQ&DJ, 124 (January 1994): 68-72. Wilson revisited Dieppe and studied the situation; the circumstances of mid-1942 in the European/Atlantic War must be considered, e.g., various pressures from Beaverbrook, America, and Russia; Montgomery was originally responsible but reversed his position; the Canadian commander, McNaughton, assumed responsibility; it was tempting but unfair to blame Mountbatten; the scapegoat was Canadian Hamilton Roberts who was never reemployed.

427 -------. "Mountbatten: Enigma in India." AQ&DJ, 116 (July 1986): 329-32. Concluded Mountbatten was a compulsive character, an enigma; India was the high-point of his career; Ismay: "No one else could have done it" (p. 331).

428 Windsor, Wallis Warfield, Duchess of. The Heart Has Its Reasons. NY: McKay, 1956, 372 pp. A memoir by the wife of Edward VIII; Mountbatten was closely involved with events.

429   Windsor, Edward, Duke of. <u>The King's Story: The Memoirs of the Duke of Windsor</u>. London: Cassell; NY: Putnam, 1951, 446 pp. Recollections of Edward (1894-1952); Mountbatten acted as travel companion to Edward during the 1920s and later.

430   "The Windsors: A Royal Family." <u>TV DOCUMENTARY</u>, 4 hours, a British-American productio; "the last great dynasty of Europe"; included Mountbatten.

431   Winton, John. <u>Captains and Kings: The Royal Family and the Royal Navy, 1901-1981</u>. Denbigh, Wales: Bluejacket, 1981, 114 pp. Included Kings George V, George VI, Edward VIII, the Duke of Edinburgh, Prince Charles, and Prince Andrew but not Mountbatten.

432   -------. <u>Sink the HAGURO!: The Last Destroyer Action of the Second World War</u>. Foreword by Earl Mountbatten. London: Seeley, 1979, 191 pp. A detailed account of a battle off Malaya, British destroyers sank a large Japanese cruiser, May 1945; Mountbatten lamented this "forgotten front" but defeat was turned into victory.

433   -------. <u>The War at Sea: An Anthology of Personal Experience</u>. Alt. subtitle: <u>The British Navy in World War II</u>. Intro. by Earl Mountbatten. London: Hutchinson; NY: Morrow, 1967, 436 pp. A year-by-year, 1939-1945, presentation of the operations of the Royal Navy during the war.

434   Wolpert, Stanley A. <u>Jinnah of Pakistan</u>. NY: Oxford UP, 1984, 433 pp. The definitive study of the life and times of Jinnah, leader of the Muslim League and the new Pakistan; exhaustively researched.

435   -------. <u>Nehru: A Tryst with History</u>. London: Oxford UP, 1997, 546 pp. A new and definitive biography of Nehru, leader of the Congress Party and the new India; details on the relationship between Nehru and Lady Mountbatten, plus Claire Booth Luce and even Jackie Kennedy.

436   Woods, John E. "The Royal Navy since World War II." <u>NIPROC</u>, 108 (March 1982): 82-90. Use of a pen name for a naval historian; a review of salient features of the Royal Navy between 1945-1981, the year of a major review by the Thatcher government, reducing naval strength--a year before the Falklands/Malvinas campaign; in August 1945 there were 990 major combat units; in the interim grandiose plans to build 4 super-carriers (none built) and 17 nuclear attack submarines, later 5 ballistic missile nuclear submarines (those also reduced); thus, continuous reductions; Mountbatten was the most identifiable naval leader for the first half of this period.

437 Woolgar, Christopher M. and Robson, K., eds. A Guide to the Archive and Manuscript Collections of the Hartley Library University of Southampton. Occasional Paper # 11, MSS 1-200. Southampton: US Library, 1992, 205 pp. A survey of the holdings of the Special Collections Division, Hartley Library; most acquisitions since 1983, e.g., Wellington, Palmerston, Mountbatten, and Anglo-Jewry papers; pertinent are the Broadlands archives including the following groups: Palmerston, Baron Mount Temple (father of Lady Mountbatten), the Mountbatten family, and Cassel papers (grandfather of Lady Mountbatten); the Mountbatten family papers included 250,000 documents and 50,000 photos; papers of Earl and Lady Mountbatten, Combined Operations, SAC SEAC, Viceroy of India, Governor-General, a separate collection on HMA KELLY, and the German branch of the family including the Marquess of Milford Haven.

438 Worswick, Clark and Embree, Ainslie. The Last Empire: Photography in British India, 1855-1911. Preface by Earl Mountbatten. London: Fraser, 1976, 149 pp. Folio size with B/W photographs; the catalogue for an Exhibition of the Asian Society, Asia House Gallery, Asia Society, summer of 1976; a delightful and nostalgic series of photographs of the life in the Raj during the late 19th century; Mountbatten noted that his father (1875-1876), brother (1911-1912), and he (1921-1922 and 1947-1948) had all visited India.

439 Wright, Bruce S. The Frogmen of Burma: The Story of the Sea Reconnaissance Unit. Foreword by Earl Mountbatten. Tornoto: Irvin, 1968, 167 pp. By a Royal Canadian Navy officer about operational swimmers formed by Wright and used in the Burma campaign, e.g., crossing the Irrawaddy River and in Ceylon; the idea came from successes of Italian frogmen in the Mediterranean Sea.

440 Young, Kenneth. The Diaries of Sir Robert Bruce Lockhart. 2 vols. London: Macmillan, 1973-1980. Lockhart (1887-1970) was a prominent official in the British government; numerous references to Mountbatten.

441 Young, Peter. Storm from the Sea. London: Kimber; Annapolis: NIP, 1958, 1989, 236 pp. A memoir of a Brig. General, British Army, about Number 3 Commando Unit and a series of amphibious landings during the war, e.g., Dieppe (pp58-74) and Burma (pp. 203-20; Young served in COHQ.

442   Ziegler, Philip, ed. The Diaries of Lord Louis Mountbatten, 1920-1922: Tours with the Prince of Wales. Foreword by Earl Mountbatten. London and NY: Collins, 1987, 1989, 315 pp. Mountbatten diaries while a companion to Edward, Prince of Wales aboard HMS RENOWN, a battlecruiser, to New Zealand, Australia, Japan, and India; Mountbatten became engaged in India.

443   -------, ed. From Shore to Shore: The Final Years: The Diaries of Earl Mountbatten of Burma, 1953-1979. London: Collins, 1989, 414 pp. A continuation of a series of diaries of Mountbatten; episodes in this one included service as commander of the Mediterranean fleet, a tour of India as 1st Sea Lord, a visit to the White House, a ride on USS SKIPJACK, a nuclear, submarine with Admiral Hyman Rickover, and his retirement; called "tour diaries."

444   -------. King Edward VIII: A Biography. Alt. subtitle: The Official Biography. London: Collins; NY: Knopf, 1990, 1991, 566 pp. Unrestricted access to the royal archives; the official biography of a controversial king who abdicated and flirted with the Nazis, who remained an immature, confused man; numerous references to the Mountbattens.

445   -------. Mountbatten: The Official Biography. London: Collins; NY: Knopf, 1985, 784 pp. The official biography of Mountbatten by the official biographer, originally to be C.S. Forester, but his death led to Ziegler being selected; unrestricted access to the personal archives; chronological division into 5 chapters; consistently candid, elaborating on faults: vain, ambitious, snob, and virtues: generous, loyal, considerate, and tolerant; Montgomery should be blamed for Dieppe, Slim did the fighting in Burma, Attlee made an inspired choice of the last Viceroy, and Nehru the choice of Governor-General; Mountbatten opposed the Suez operation and the independent nuclear force; his funeral, minutely planned by Mountbatten, was opportunity for a national catharsis; a model for official biography.

446   -------. Mountbatten Revisited. British Studies Distinguished Lecture series # 27. Austin: U Tex P, n.d. A special lecture presenting an assessment of Mountbatten to an audience at the University of Texas.

447   -------, ed. Personal Diary of Admiral the Lord Louis Mountbatten: Supreme Allied Commander South-East Asia, 1943-1946. No publication information. Another in the series of diaries of Mountbatten, this one while SAC SEAC.

448   -------. "Review of Brian Loring Villa, Unauthorized Action." Spectator, 264 (10 March 1990). Villa was revisionist and critical of

Mountbatten; Ziegler was an apologist for Mountbatten; stimulated some correspondence in subsequent issues.

449   Zuckerman, Lord Solly. The Autobiography of Solly Zuckerman. 2 vols. London: Hamilton; NY: Norton, 1978-1988, 946 pp. Zuckerman was an academic, expert science advisor, government official, and arms negotiator; his speciality was Anglo-American relations; involved in the procurement of Polaris; many references to "Dickie."

450   -------. Six Men Out of the Ordinary. London: Owen, 1992, 200 pp. Foreword by the Duke of Edinburgh; profiles of 6 exceptional men, 3 English and 3 Americans including Lord Arthur Tedder, Carl Spaatz, Rickover, and Mountbatten (pp. 131-68); "the man of all ambitions. . . . The quintessential admiral"; Zuckerman joined COHQ staff as scientific advisor; some expose, e.g., Mountbatten figured in the Cecil King Affair, an effort to use clandestine means to replace Prime Minister Harold Wilson with a coalition goverment headed by Mountbatten; Zuckerman claimed he persuaded Mountbatten to withdraw from the effort; claims and rumors that Mountbatten was a homosexual and Soviet spy were groundless; in retirement, Mountbatten did "rewrite history," i.e., some embellishment and imagination added.

Author Index

NOTE: Page numbers are in roman type; bibliographical entries are in italics.

Adamthwaite, Anthony, 47, *1*
Akbar, Ahmed, 41, *2-3*
Al Din Quraishi, Salim, *50*
Albert, J.G., 47, *4*
Aldgate, Anthony, 24, *5*
Ali, Chaudri Muhammad, 42, *6*
Allen, Louis, 33, 35-6, *7-10*
Allen, Ralph, 29, *11*
Al-Solami, D.A., 47, *12*
Aronson, Theo, 17, *13*
Aspinall-Oglander, Cecil F., 26, *14*
Atherton, Louise, 6, *15*
Atkin, Ronald, 29, *16*
Austin, Alexander B., 29, *17*
Azad, Maulana Abul Kalam, 40, *18*

Baker, George E., 14, *19*
Baker, Richard, 46, 55, *20-1*
Ball, S.J., 46, *22*
Ballard, George A., 55, *23*
Barclay, Glen St. John, 27, *24*

Barker, A.J., 35, 47, *25-6*
Barnett, Correlli, 22, *27*
Barratt, John, 14, *28*
Barris, Alex, *29*
Barris, Ted, 29, *29*
Bartlett, Merrill L., 27, *30*
Beamish, Derek, 55, *31*
Beaufre, Andre, 47, *32*
Beaumont, Roger A., 27-8, *33-4*
Beesly, Patrick, 55, *35*
Belsky, Frank, 54, *36*
Bidwell, Shelford, 35, *37*
Bond, Brian, 10, *38*
Boothroyd, Basil, 19, *39*
Bradford, Sarah, 19, *40*
Bramall, Lord Dwin, *193*
Brecher, Michael, 42, *41*
Brewer, James F., 34, *42*
Broadbent, Sir Ewen, 47, *43*
Brookshire, Jerry H., 43, *45*
Brown, David, 46, *46*
Brown, Judith M., 40, *47*
Bryant, Sir Arthur, 32, *48*
Buckley, Christoper, 29, *49*
Burke, Samuel M., 40, *50*

Butler, David, 14, *52*

Callahan, Raymond A., 35,
 53
Calvert, Michael, 35, *54*
Campbell, John P., 29, *55*
Campbell-Johnson, Alan, 14,
 16, 41, *56*
Canella, Charles J., 32, *57*
Cannadine, David, 19, *58*
Canning, John, 15, *59*
Carter, April, 11, *60*
Cartland, Barbara, 9, 55, *61-
 2*
Carver, Michael, 15, *63-4*
Castle, Charles, 14, *65*
Charmley, John, 46, *68*
Churchill, Randolph, *142*
Clifford, Kenneth J., 27, *69*
Collins, Larry, 42, *70-1*
Connell, Brian, 18, *75*
Connell, G.G., 23-4, *76*
Controvich, James T., 1, 11,
 77
Cookbridge, E.H., 18, *78-9*
Copland, Ian, 41, *80*
Corfield, Sir Conrad, 41, *81*
Coultass, Clive, 24, *82*
Coupland, Reginald, 40, *83-
 4*
Coward, Noel, 9, 14, *85-6*
Cras, Herve, 29, *87*
Cross, John P., 38, *88*
Crowe, William J., 46, *89*

Darby, Phillip G.C., *90-1*
Darwin, John, 39, *92*
Das, Manmath Nath, 41, *93*
Davie, Michael, 9, *94*
Davies, John P., Jr., 34, *95*
Deacon, Richard, 50, *96*

Dennis, Peter, 33, *97*
Dimbleby, Jonathan, 20, *100*
Donnison, F.S.V., *101*
Dooley, Howard J., 47, *102*
Dorril, Stephen, 49, *103*
Douglas, W.A.B., 10, *104*
Drummond, Malden, 55, *105*
Dunn, Peter M., 37, *106-7*
Dupuy, Trevor N., 15, *108*
Durnford-Slater, John, 28,
 109

Eakins, T.G., 55, *110*
Eden, Anthony, Earl of
 Avon, 47, *111*
Edwardes, Michael, 40, 42,
 112-3
Eiler, Keith E., 35, *114*
Embree, Ainslie, *438*
Evans, Sir Geoffrey C., 35,
 117
Evans, William, 14, *118*

Fairbanks, Douglas, Jr., 9,
 119-21
Faligot, Roger, 50, *122*
Fay, Peter Ward, 32, *123*
Fergusson, Sir Bernard E.,
 27, 35, *124-5*
Fischer, Edward, 31, *126*
Fisher, Clive, 14, *127*
Fjellman, Margit, 18, *128*
Flamini, Roland, 19, *129*
Florence, Arnold, 3, *130*
Foot, M.R.D., 29, *131*
Forester, Cecil Scott, 5, 12,
 132
Franks, Norman L.R., 29,
 133
Fuller, Edward, 55, *134*
Fullick, Roy, 47, *135*

Galatin, I.J., 46, *136*
Gardiner, Juliet, 52, *138*
Garlock, Peter David, 40, *139*
Garrett, Richard, 28, 49, *140-1*
Gilbert, Martin, *142*
Giuseppi, Montagu S., 6, *143*
Glendevon, Baron John Hope, 43, *144*
Gooch, John, 47, *145*
Gopal, Sarvepalli, 42-3, *146*
Gracey, Sir Douglas, 8, *147*
Greenhous, Brereton, *104*
Grigg, John, 42, *148*
Gueritz, E.F., 24, *149*

Halpern, Paul G., 8, 22, *150-1*
Hamid, S. Shahid, 40, *152*
Hamilton, Nigel, 27, *153*
Hampshire, A. Cecil, 17, 46, *154-5*
Hankins, Cyril, 18, *156*
Harris, Kenneth, 15, 42, *157-8*
Harwood, David, 55, *159*
Hasler, H.G., *327*
Hastings, Stephen L.E., 46, *160*
Hatch, Alden, 18, *161*
Heald, Tim, 19, *162*
Henry, Hugh G., 29, *163*
Henshaw, Peter J., 29-30, *164-5*
Higham, Charles, 19, *166*
Higham, Robin, 10-1, *167-9*
Hill, J.R., 22, *170*
Hoare, Philip, 14, *171*
Hoey, Brian, 13, *172*

Holman, Dennis, 16, *173*
Horan, David W., 28, *174*
Horan, H.E., 28, *175*
Hough, Richard A., 8, 13, 16, 18-9, 23, *176-81*
Howard, Sir Michael, 47, *182*
Howarth, Stephen, 22, *183*
Htin Aung, U., 36, *184*
Hudson, Henry V., 40, *185*
Hughes, Edward Arthur, 22, *186*
Hughes-Hallett, J., 27, *187*
Humphrey-Smith, Cecil, 55, *188*
Hunter, Charles N., 35, *189*
Hunter, T. Murray, 30, *190*

Inder Singh, Anita, 40, *191*

Jackson, Sir William, 47, *193*
Jalal, Ayesha, 43, *194*
Johnson, Franklyn A., 47, *195-8*
Johnson, Roy Frank, 55, *199*
Jordan, Gerald, 11, 21, 29, *200*
Judd, Denis, 19, *201*

Kadel, Robert J., 34, *202*
Kemp, Peter, *203*
Kent, Barrie, 22, *204*
Kerr, Mark Edward Fredric, 18, *205*
Keyes, Lord Roger, 8, 27, *206-7*
King, Norman, 55, *208*
Kirby, S. Woodburn, 10, 35, 55, *209-10*
Kiriakopoulos, G.C., 23, *211*

Kirkpatrick, Lyman B., Jr.,
    30, *212*
Krishan, Y., 41, *213*
Kyi, Aung San Suu, 36, *214*
Kyle, Keith, 47, *215*

Ladd, James D., 28, *216-7*
Lahr, John, *218*
Lambton, Antony, 18, *219*
Lane, Peter, 19, *220*
Langdon, Jeremy, 27, *221*
Lapierre, Dominique, *70-1*
Law, Derek G., 11, *223*
Leasor, James, 29, 34, *224-5*
Lee, Loyd E., 10, *226*
Leigh, Vida, 55, *227*
Lepotier, Adolphe Auguste
    Marie, 28, *228*
Lesley, Cole, 14, *229-30*
Lewin, Ronald, 26, 35, *231-
3*
Lewin, Sir Terrence, 51, *235*
Lider, Julian, 46, *234*
Lieven, D.C.B., 17, *236*
Liversidge, Douglas, 18, *238*
Lockhart, Sir Robert Bruce,
    28, *239*
Lonn, George, 54, *240*
Lorelli, John A., 28, *241*
Lucas, W. Scott, 47, *242-4*

Macartney-Filgate, Terence,
    423
MacBeth, George, 52, *245*
McDonald, Kendall, 55, *246*
McGeoch, Sir Ian, *247-8*
McInnes, Colin J., 46, *249*
Macintyre, Donald G.F.W.,
    32, *250*
Macksey, Kenneth, 51, *251*
Maguire, Eric, 29, *252*

Manning, Thomas D., 24,
    254
Mansergh, Nicholas, 40, *255*
March, Edgar J., 24, *256*
MARCO, 49, *257-8*
Marder, Arthur J., 22, *259*
Marx, Roland, 50, *260*
Mason, David, 28, 51, *261-2*
Masson, Madeline, 16, *263*
Matthews, Geoffrey F., 35,
    264
Maund, L.E.H., 27, *265*
Maung, U. Maung, 36, *266*
Menon, V.P., 40, *267-8*
Messenger, Charles, 28, *269*
Miall, Leonard, 55, *270*
Millar, George, 27, *271*
Millington-Drake, Sir
    Eugene, 24, *272*
Mitchell, L.M., 5-6, *273*
Moir, Martin, 6, *274*
Moncrieff, Anthony, 47, *275*
Moon, Sir Penderel, 40, *276*
Moore, R.J., 40-1, 43, *277-9*
Morgan, Janet P., 6, 16, *280*
Moseley, Roy, *166*
Mosley, Leonard, 41, *281*
Mountbatten, Edwina
    Cynthia Annette, 6, *297-8*
Mountbatten, Louis
    Alexander, 21, *299*
Mountbatten, Louis Francis
    Albert Victor Nicholas,
    300-2
Mountbatten of Burma, Earl,
    6, 8, 13, 18, 29, 33, 41,
    49-50, *282-96*
Murfett, Malcolm, 46-7, *304*
Murphy, Ray Livingston,
    14, *305*

Nailor, Peter, 46, *306*
Navias, Martin S., 45-6,
307-8
Nelson, Hank, 34, *309*

Olver, A.S.B., 33, *310*
Owen, Charles, 22, *311*
Owen, Frank, 35, *312*
Owen, N.J., 43, *313*

Pack, Stanley W.C., 23, *314*
Palmer, Alan W., 17, 51,
316-7
Pandey, B.N., 33, 38, *318-9*
Parker, John, 19, *320*
Parkes, Oscar, 24, *321*
Patterson, A. Temple, 6, *322*
Pattinson, William, 23, *323*
Payn, Graham, 14, *324*
Pearson, Michael, *386*
Philip, Duke of Edinburgh,
325
Philips, C.H., 40, *326*
Phillips, Cecil E.L., 28, *327-
9*
Phillips, Lucas, 35
Pierre, Andrew J., 46, *330*
Poolman, Kenneth, 23, *331*
Post, Laurens van der, 37,
332
Powell, Geoffrey, *135*
Prather, Russel E., 35, *333*
Pratt, Marjorie Minna, 16,
334

Ramsay, Robin, *103*
Ramsey, W.G., 29, *336*
Rasor, Eugene L., 1, 11,
337-41
Reed, Bruce, 48, *342*
Rees, Wyn, 45, *343*

Reyburn, Wallace, 29, *344*
Reynolds, Quentin, 29, *345*
Rhodes James, Robert, 47,
346
Richards, Jeffrey, *5*
Ritchie, Jean, *28*
Rizvi, Gowher, 43, *347*
Roberts, Hugh A., 3, *348*
Robson, K., *437*
Rockwell, Theodore, 46, *349*
Romanus, Charles F., 34,
350-1
Rooney, D. David, 35, *352-3*
Rose, Kenneth, 19, *354*
Roskill, Stephen W., 10, 22,
30, *355-6*
Ross, Al, 24, *357*
Royle, Trevor, 35, *358*

Sbrega, John J., 32, *359*
Seervai, Hormasji M., 40,
360
Sherwani, Latif A., 42, *361*
Shuckburgh, Evelyn, 47, *362*
Simpson, John, 46, *363*
Simpson, Michael, 8, *364*
Slim, Sir William, 35, *365*
Smith, Charles, 14, *366*
Smith, Simon C., 37, *367*
Smurthwaite, David, 31, *368*
Snyder, William P., 46, *369-
70*
Spector, Ronald H., 31, *372-
3*
Spoto, Donald, 18, *374*
Squire, Clifford W., 37, *375*
Stacey, C.P., 10, 29, *376-7*
Stannard, Martin, 14, *378*
Steers, H.J.T., 26, *379*
Stephen, Martin, 22, *380*
Sternlicht, Sanford V., 12,

381
Stilwell, Joseph W., 8, *382*
Strange, Joseph L., 27, *383*
Strong, Charles L., 55, *384-5*
Strutton, Bill, *386*
Sunderland, Riley, *350-1*
Sweetman, John, 47, *387*
Swettenham, John, 30, *388*
Swinson, Arthur, 13, *389*

Talbot, I.A., 41, *390*
Tarling, Nicholas, 33, 36, *391-3*
Taylor, A.J.P., 15, *394*
Teed, Peter, 51, *395*
Terraine, John, 13, *396-7*
Terry, Thurzal Q., 34, *398*
Thomas, David A., 23, 28, *399-400*
Thomas, Hugh, 47, *401*
Thompson, Julian, 34, *402*
Thorne, Christopher G., 31, *403-4*
Tinker, Hugh, 36, 42, *405-8*
Tiratsoo, Nick, 43, *409*
Trenowden, Ian, *410*
Tuchman, Barbara W., 34, *411*

Villa, Brian Loring, 28, 30, 56, *412-3*

Wainwright, Mary D., *326*
Walker, C.F., *254*
Warner, Oliver, 14, *414*
Warner, Philip, 43, *415*
Watson, Francis, 43, *416*

Wavell, Archibald, Earl, 43, *417*
Werstein, Irving, 14, *418*
Wheeler, Nicholas J., 46, *419*
Wheeler-Bennett, John W., 19, *420*
Whitaker, Denis, 29, *422*
Whitaker, Shelagh, *422*
Whitehead, William, 29, *423*
Williams, Geoffrey, *342*
Willmott, H.P., 32, *424-5*
Wilson, Sir James, 29, 41, *426-7*
Windsor, Edward, Duke of, *429*
Windsor, Wallis Warfield, Duchess of, *428*
Winton, John, 17, 22, 24, *431-3*
Wolpert, Stanley A., 42-3, *434-5*
Woodhouse, William, *251*
Woods, John E., 46, *436*
Woolgar, Christopher M., 5, *437*
Worswick, Clark, 55, *438*
Wright, Bruce S., 55, *439*

Young, Kenneth, 10, *440*
Young, Peter, 28, *441*

Ziegler, Philip, 3, 5-6, 8, 12-3, 15, 19, 23, 28, 30, 40-1, *442-8*
Zuckerman, Lord Solly, 10, 49, 51, *449-50*

Subject Index

Admiral of the Sea, 22
American
  nuclear deterrent position,
    4, 45-46
  role in war, 28-30
  Suez, 46-47
amphibious warfare, 26-27
Anti-Facist People's Freedom
  League, 36
archives, 5-6
Ashley, Edwina, 3
Ashley, W. W., 5
Asian/Pacific war, 1, 10, 31-38
Atlee, Clement, 40-41, 43
Auchinlech, Claude, 40
Australia, 10, 31, 34
Australian War Memorial, 7

Balkan peninsula, 23
Battenberg, Prince Louis of, 3, 5,
  14, 18, 21
Beatty, David, 3
Beaverbrook, Lord, 15, 20, 24, 29-
  30
Beresford, Lord, 18
Britain
  China-Burma-India, 31-38
  Dieppe, 29-30
  India, 39-41

  nuclear deterrent, 45-46
  Suez, 46-47
British Library, 7
Broadlands, 54
Broadlands Archive, 3, 5-6, 12-13,
  16, 18
Bruneval, 27
Burke, Arleigh, 45
Burma, 31, 34-37

Cairo Conference, 4, 34
Cambodia, 36-37
Canada, 4, 10, 28-31, 49-50
Cartland, Barbara, 9
Casablanca Conference, 4
Cassel, Edward, 5, 18
Central Pacific campaign, 1, 11
Charles, Prince, 4, 10, 20, 56
Chennault, Claire, 32
Chiang Kai-shek, 31
Chief of Defence Staff, 4, 47-48
China, 31
China-Burma-India campaign, 1,
  8, 21, 31-38
China-Burma-India Hump Pilots
  Association, 34
CHINDITS, 10, 32, 35
Churchill Archives, 7
Churchill, Winston, 4, 10, 17, 19-

20, 22, 26, 29, 32, 39-40, 42
Combined Chiefs of Staff, 32-33
Combined Operations Head-
   quarters (COHQ), 22, 24, 26-28
commandos, 27-28
Commonwealth, 31
Congress Party, 39, 41-42
Coward, Noel, 9, 14, 23-24
Crete, 23-24
Cripps, Stafford, 40

decolonization, 33, 39-40
Defence White Paper of 1958, 45
Denmark, 23
Dieppe, 4, 6, 9, 21, 27-30, 52
Dorman-Smith, Reginald, 36

Eden, Anthony, 46-47
Edward VIII, King, 3, 4, 8, 19
Egypt, 46-47
Eisenhower, Dwight, 32
Elizabeth, Queen, 4
European/Atlantic war, 10

5th Destroyer Flotilla, 23
40th anniversary, 30
50th anniversary, 30
Fairbanks, Douglas, 9
Far East, 31-38
First Vietnam War, 37
Forester, C.S., 12
France
   Indochina, 36-37
   role in World War II, 29
   Suez, 46-47
Frogmore House, 3

Gandhi, Mahatma, 11, 40-41, 43
George V, King, 19
George VI, King, 4, 19
Germany
   archives, 7
   Dieppe, 34

role in World War II, 23-24, 28-
   30
Giffard, 34
Gracey, Douglas, 8, 37
GRAF SPEE, 24
Greece, 23

Hartley Library, 5-6
Healey, Dennis, 48
Hesse, 3, 17
Hicks, Lady Pamela, 16, 51
Higham, Robin, 10-11
HMS ILLUSTRIOUS, 21, 26
HMS KASHIMIR, 23
HMS KELLY, 4, 23-24, 26
HMS KIPLING, 23
HMS JERVIS, 23
HMS LION, 3, 21, 50
HMS QUEEN ELIZABETH, 3
Hough, Richard, 8, 13, 16
House of Hanover, 3
House of Windsor, 3
Hughes-Hallet, 6

Imperial War Museum, 7, 51
"In Which We Serve", 23-24
India, 4, 6, 10, 17, 31-32, 36, 39-
   44
India Office Library and Records,
   6
Indochina, 33, 36-37
Indonesia, 37
Irish Republican Army (IRA), 4,
   50
Isle of Wight, 3
Israel, 46-47
Italy, 23

Japan, 31-39
Japanese Home Islands, 31
Jinnah, Mohammed Ali, 40-44

KELLY Reunion Association, 23,

33-34
Kennedy, John, 46
Kew, Richmond, United Kingdom,
   6
Keyes, Roger, 8, 26-27
King, Cecil, 49, 56

Laos, 36-37
LeFanu, Michael, 48
Liddell Hart Centre, 8
Linlithgow, Lord, 40, 43
Lockhard, Robert Bruce, 10
Long Range Penetration Group,
   32, 35

MacArthur, Douglas, 1, 10-11, 32-
   33, 56
Macmillan, Harold, 46
Malaya, 37-38
manuscript collection, 5
MARCO, 49
Marder, Arthur, 22
Marquess of Milford Haven, 3
Marshall, George, 28-29
McGeoch, Ian, 46
Mediterranean, 23-24
Merrill's Marauders, 35
Ministry of Defence, 21, 47-48
Ministry of Defence Headquarters
   Libraries, 7
Morgan, Janet, 16
Mountbatten, Admiral of the Fleet
   the Right Honorable Louis
   Francis Albert Victor Nicholas
      addresses, 54
      Anglo-American relations, 34
      assassination, 4, 50
      author, 49-50
      assessments of, 3, 50-52
      awards, 52-53
      Battenberg, 3, 17-18
      bibliographies, 10-11
      biographies, 8-9, 10-16, 41

birthplace, 3
Burma, 35-36
Chief of Combined Operations,
   4, 26
Chief of Staff of the Defence
   Forces, 4, 47-48
China, 1, 11, 34
China-Burma-India campaign,
   1, 31-38
commands, 4
correspondence, 6
death, 4, 13, 50
diaries, 8, 10
"Dickie", 3
Dieppe, 4, 27-30, 56
documentaries, 9, 13-14, 41, 51
education, 3
family, 4
First Sea Lord of the
   Admiralty, 4, 21, 45-48
forewords, 55
future research, 56
Hanoverian connection, 17
HMS KELLY, 23-24
homosexual allegations, 13, 51
India, 4, 39-44
Indonesia, 37
influences, 4
introductions, 55
Japanese surrender, 33
lineage, 3, 7, 17-20, 56
lifestyle, 13, 19, 49-51
Malaya, 37-38
MARCO, 49
marriage, 3-4. See also,
   Mountbatten, Lady Edwina
Ministry of Defence, 21
movies, 23-24
nicknames, 3, 53-54
novels, 14
nuclear deterrent, 4, 45-46, 56
official histories, 10

pamphlets, 55-56
papers, 3, 5-11
parents, 3
polo, 49
portraits, 53
prison investigation, 49
retirement, 49
Royal Air Force, 26
Royal family, 17-20, 56
Royal Navy, 11, 17-18, 21-26,
    45-48
ships, 3
Souheast Asia, 31-38
statues, 54
Suez crisis, 4, 46-47
summit conferences, 4
Supreme Allied Command, 1,
    4, 8, 31-38, 45
titles, 3, 52-53
unification of services, 47-48
Viceroy and Governor General
    of India, 4, 26, 45
Windsor, 17, 19-20
World War I, 22
World War II, 23, 25-38
Mountbatten Center for
  International Studies, 3, 6
Mountbatten, Lady Edwina, 3, 4,
  9
  biographies, 12, 16, 18
  future research, 56
  India, 40, 42-43
  papers, 5-6
  portraits, 54
  titles and honors, 53
Mountbatten, Louise, 18
Mountbatten Memorial Lecture
  Series, 51
Mountbatten, Patricia, 4, 51
Muslim League, 41, 43

Nassar, President, 46-47
Nassau Agreement, 46

National Archives, 7
Nehru, Jawaharlal, 6, 40, 42, 44
Nehru Memorial Trust, 42
New Zealand, 31
Nimitz, Chester, 2, 11, 32
North Africa, 23
nuclear deterrent, 4, 45-46

official histories, 10
OPERATION CHARIOT, 28
OPERATION JUBILEE, 52
OPERATION MASTERDOM, 37
Osborne House, 3

Pacific Ocean Area, 2, 32
Pakistan, 43
Palmerston, Lord, 3, 5
Patel, Sadar, 40
Pearce, General, 36
Philip, Duke of Edinburgh, 4, 8,
    18-19, 50, 56
Polaris ballistic missile system, 45
Potsdam Agreement, 37
Potsdam Conference, 4
Pownall, Henry, 10
prisoners of war, 33-34
Public Record Office, 6

Quebec Conference, 4, 32

Raj, 39
Rickover, Hyman, 45-46
River Plate, 24
Roosevelt, Franklin Delano, 32,
    36, 39-40
Roskill, Stephen, 22, 30
Royal Archives, 5, 7
Royal family, 17
Royal Naval College, 22
Royal Navy, 9, 17-18, 21-25, 45-
    48
Royal United Services Institute for
    Defence Studies, 7

Russia, 28

San, Aung, 36
signals, 22
Singapore, 31
Slim, William, 35
Society of Naval Research, 50
Solomon Islands campaign, 2
Somerville, James, 8, 22, 32
Southeast Asia Command, 10, 31
Southwest Pacific campaign, 1,
    10-11, 32
St. Nazaire, 28
Stilwell, Joseph, 8, 32-35
Suez, 4, 46-47
Suez Canal, 46-47
Supreme Allied Commander,
Southeast Asia Command, 1, 22,
    31-38

Truman, Harry S., 36

U, Nu, 36

United States, 7, 33-37
University of Southampton, 3, 5

Viceroy to India, 42
Vichy France, 36
Victoria of Hesse, 3
Victoria, Queen, 3, 17
Vietnam, 8, 36-37

Waugh, Evelyn, 9, 14
Wavell, Earl, 40, 43
"Way Ahead Committee", 46
Wellington papers, 6
Whitehall Yard, 7
Wingate, Orde, 10, 32, 35
World War I, 21
World War II, 3, 5, 21
Windsor, 3, 17-18

Yugoslavia, 23

Ziegler, Philip, 12

About the Author

EUGENE L. RASOR, who is retired, was professor of history at Emory and Henry College. He has compiled several bibliographies, including most recently, *China-Burma-India Campaign, 1941–1945: Historiography and Annotated Bibliography* (Greenwood, 1998) and *The Soloman Islands Campaign, Guadalcanal to Rabaul: Historiography and Annotated Bibliography* (Greenwood, 1997).